Broken ANGELS

Broken ANGELS

Breaking the chains of
domestic abuse

ABIGAIL SINCLAIR

Sarah GRACE PUBLISHING

First published in 2017 by Sarah Grace Publishing, an imprint of
Malcolm Down Publishing Ltd.

www.malcolmdown.co.uk

British Library Cataloguing in Publication Data
A catalogue record for this book is available from the British Library.

ISBN 978-1-910786-83-3

Art Direction and photography by Sarah Grace
Additional design by Esther Kotecha

Printed in Malta

Contents

DEDICATION

This book is dedicated to the most amazing support network
any woman could ever have.
And to my late uncle, my hero.

Endorsement

'A moving and inspiring account of survival and the author's amazing strength, this will help so many women, especially those who are about to take that first terrifying step towards freedom.'

Pat Craven
Freedom Programme

THE JUMP

When you were a child, did you ever climb on a wall and walk along it as it got higher and higher? Others who had gone on ahead would jump off and then they would encourage you to do so, but you were scared?

Maybe you were one of the brave ones who just jumped down. But you could have been one of the ones just like me, who would dither and tremble and wait until I'd talked myself out of it and then slowly make my way back to where the wall was lower and step off.

Well, I guess what I am trying to say is that was what it was like. All those years I kept turning round and choosing to take the easy steps back rather than risk the jump, each and every time hating myself just that little bit more for not having the guts to jump.

Something told me that this time I could not turn back, that the wall behind me had been blown up, so my only choice was to jump. I thought the jump was the hardest part but soon became aware that it was just the start.

Once I jumped off I went into 'Operation: Get Me Out'. Like some bizarre maze, stretching for thousands of miles, I embarked on a journey which was exhausting, but I knew there was only one exit and I just needed to be patient and focus until I found it. I pray that this book will educate and inspire others to escape their own torture and set themselves free.

INTRODUCTION

Here's to strong women.
May we know them.
May we be them.
May we raise them.

I have chosen to write the following journal in the hope that it will inspire others to remove themselves from relationships that are clouded by domestic abuse.

I have had the privilege of residing in a women's refuge with my daughter, and I hope this account will challenge and remove the many stigmas attached to life in a refuge which, although unusual and at times hard, can only be described as an incredible healing journey.

I hope this journal will give a glimpse of refuge life and will spread the word that there really is a place where people can escape to. A place that is safe and clean, offering incredible support, guidance and boundaries. A place where women and their children can rest a while and begin to fix their broken lives and dreams, until it's time to move on . . .

My ultimate wish is to address the effects that domestic abuse has on children. Poor little prisoners swept along, learning to brave the unpredictable tides of domestic abuse. Their acute senses alerting them, day in, day out, to the storms looming, growing, gathering force and yet they are never quite sure when it will hit, where it will hit and what damage it will leave behind.

I was horrified by the statistics of children living in the UK within the confines of domestic abuse and the effect it can have on them.

130,000 children live in homes where there is high-risk domestic abuse. 62% of children living with domestic abuse are directly harmed by the perpetrator of the abuse, in addition to the harm caused by witnessing the abuse of others. (St Albans and Hertsmere Women's Refuge)

My reason for writing *Broken Angels* is not to gain sympathy but a need to help others. I am a private person who is desperate to protect my daughter and myself. However, sometimes life throws up obstacles . . . things blow up in your face. Dreams are shattered in moments and I can't turn my back on a chance to help someone else.

Using some of my own experiences and turning them into something creative makes up for it all somehow.

I still hear so many people coming out with the same prejudices against people who are affected by domestic abuse: 'Those types of women'; 'Women like that'. May I say here, right now, that there really aren't any of 'those types of women'.

Living in refuge and attending the Freedom Programme course taught me that domestic abuse affects anyone. Men, women, children, siblings, parents, same sex relationships. There are wealthy women, married to doctors and lawyers. There are women from different countries who moved here with the promise of a new, safe life. There are teenage girls fleeing abusive partners or parents, and there are women who suffered for years behind the disguise of the perfect family.

This book is not written to hurt anyone or seek revenge or

retribution. It is written from my heart, in my desire to help someone, anyone, affected by domestic abuse.

By writing this book I have been able to explore the many complex layers of domestic abuse. I have been able to understand why, perhaps, my previous partner treated me the way that he did . . .

He grew up in a toxic home environment; he was also bullied at school. Had he received help when he was a child, would his behaviour have been different from how it is today? Perhaps his obsession with needing to be in control stems back to a childhood where he felt anything but in control?

For whatever reason, I bare him no malice and I hope one day he finds peace.

I will always be grateful to him for giving me my beautiful daughter. How can I not be grateful to the man who gave me something so precious?

Others have allowed me to use their experiences of domestic abuse in *Broken Angels*. They, too, are hoping that by sharing their stories they will help to break the taboos of domestic abuse and help others.

JUST

'JUST'

A small innocuous word and yet, used in certain contexts, it carries one hell of a punch!

Something that has come back to haunt me with a vengeance recently is people's opinions and attitude towards me when I was living in an abusive relationship. People would say:

'Why don't you **JUST** . . ?'
'If it was me, I would **JUST** . . ?'
'I would tell him to **JUST** get out.'
'I'd **JUST** leave. I would never put my kids through that.'

All of them thought they were helping but, in truth, they made me feel so much less of a woman than any of them. Their declarations of their own strength and intolerance crushed me; I became psychologically even smaller than I already felt.

These were the people close to me. These were the ones who loved me, and if they had no understanding then how on earth could I expect others to understand?

I didn't blame them for feeling as they did. How could I when I didn't really understand any of it myself? If I'm honest, because it had been so slow, so subtle. I guess I didn't see it until it had completely consumed me.

Until you have lived in an abusive relationship it is perhaps difficult for you to be able to see why people don't 'JUST leave and walk out.'

'So, why didn't I leave and JUST walk out?'

I Didn't Get It

I have tried making sense of this myself . . .

He never hit me but I wish he had.

I wish he had punched me and kicked me until I was black and blue and hospitalised. Perhaps then I wouldn't have stayed quiet for so long. Anything would have been better than that never ending, wearing misery.

So why didn't I leave and JUST walk out?

Control

Coercive control was often used. He controlled everything.

It wasn't until everyone and everything I'd had in my life when I met my partner had gone that I started to question him.

When I was pregnant, he wanted to control what I did, where I went, who I saw and what I ate. If I got upset about the tight rein of control he held me on, he would use my unborn baby against me. I wasn't to get upset and was to 'think of the baby'.

He fielded all calls.

I missed my family.

I cried for my family.

He would allow me minimal contact. I was only allowed to call them at Christmas and on their birthdays. Eventually that, too, had to stop. He had good reasons for this. He didn't want me having anything to do with my family in case it would have some kind of effect on my unborn baby.

I did as I was told.

He took my phone away from me, reasoning that he was worried that the radiation from it would hurt our unborn child.

JUST

One night my car broke down in the pitch dark. I was terrified. I was seven-and-a-half months pregnant. There had been a horrendous storm and my car had swerved into a deep puddle. The engine died and I had to walk a long way to find houses.

Lightning flashed in the sky above me and trees creaked and swayed. Cars flew past splashing me with water. There were no street lights and I was dressed all in black. I was petrified of lightning and the dark.

I remember trying to run and screaming for God to help me. The pregnancy restricted the speed I could run but I battled on until I eventually found a small housing estate.

I went from house to house and eventually a kind lady gave me a lift home.

My ex was away working so, in the absence of all my friends and family, I had to call his mother and stepfather as I had started having contractions. I was embarrassed as we hardly knew each other back then.

They drove me to hospital and I was wired up to machines. The contractions started becoming more regular. The doctors reassured me that if the baby did arrive that night, then all should be okay, as babies were often born early. However, they needed to prepare me as 'premature babies are a little more vulnerable'.

I remember lying in the hospital bed, despising myself for risking our baby's life. I should have insisted on carrying my phone.

My ex's mother and stepfather kept asking me why I hadn't had a phone with me. The hospital staff asked why I didn't have a phone with me at seven-and-a-half months pregnant. I couldn't tell the doctors the truth; that my baby's father had forbidden me from carrying one. I did tell my ex's mother. She hadn't been at all surprised!

Fortunately the contractions ceased a few hours later and I

didn't have my baby that night.

The doctor told me off. Had I had my phone with me that night, all could have been avoided. I would have been able to get help and not run screaming down a long, dark road.

My ex allowed me to carry one after that but insisted it be switched off at all times so as not to hurt our unborn child. He said if people needed to get in touch with me then they knew his number and could get me through him.

It was his mobile number given on our landline answerphone. I wasn't allowed to answer the landline. 'If it's important, they will leave a message.'

My parents and grandparents would call begging me to phone them but I wasn't allowed.

On the rare occasions I did call them, he would sulk for days to punish me. He would be horrible and when eventually I snapped and cried, he would remind me: 'This is precisely why you must not have contact with your family. It clearly upsets you, which has a negative effect on our family.'

I would try to point out that it was he who was making me cry by not allowing me to speak to them, but he would have none of it!

He didn't like me giving my number to anyone.

When my aunt called me to tell me my grandfather was dying, I was desperate to go and see him, but my ex said that it would make me unwell which could affect our new baby.

He reminded me that I had my own family now.

My grandfather died, asking for me. I didn't go. I will never forget that and how it still makes me feel.

'So why didn't I leave and **JUST** walk out?'

Oh Silly Me, It Was All My Fault!

It seemed to me that the more I tried to please my ex, the more

I got wrong.

Having a dog was wrong . . .

He made me keep my dog outside in a shed. When I cried and begged him to let the dog come in he would sulk and start scratching, saying the dog made him ill.

Most of the meals I cooked were wrong . . .

He would spit out my food in front of our daughter and shout at me. It was too hot. It was too tough. There wasn't enough meat. It was the wrong meat. It didn't have enough vegetables. There were too many vegetables and 'what was he, a rabbit?'

My food made him ill.

It wasn't right.

It was all wrong.

The arguments were reaching worrying heights. Our beautiful, innocent daughter was beginning to be affected. To avoid arguing I took my psychotherapist's advice and would try to get out of the house as much as possible. When meal times became intolerable, I knew I had to remove myself further.

He told me that the house was harmonious when I wasn't there. He told me that his foul moods and temper didn't exist when I was away. He would tell my daughter and me that I was the cause of his bad temper. So, I would remove myself.

So why didn't I leave and **JUST** walk out?

I tried . . .

Escape

I would beg him to get out of the house more, to help dilute the awful toxic cloud we were living under, but unless he was working he refused to leave the house and made it clear he would never move out.

So . . . I would escape to my parents three days a week. This helped as he worked weekends and we had respite. We would only have to be in the same house maybe one or two days a week. I would return home just as he was due to leave for work.

My respite was at a huge cost.

People talked.

People questioned: 'How could a mother leave her nine-year-old daughter three days a week?'

Guilt tortured me more than the misery. One of my closest friends sent me an aggressive text, telling me: 'Wake up and come back, your daughter needs you. This isn't about you. You are an adult. Your daughter needs you to be at home.'

It's funny how her words still haunt me today. Part of me agreed with her. However . . .

My long-term mental health issues were coming back with a vengeance and the worse I got, the more ammunition he had to use against me.

My father called my ex's mother. He was desperately worried about me as I was becoming more and more anxious. Weight was falling off me daily.

My father pointed out that the house had been given to me, and that my ex had money, whilst I didn't, so why wouldn't he move out?

My ex's mother told my father that there was no way her son would give up our council house. She also pointed out that, as far as she was concerned, I no longer lived at the house as I chose to stay with my parents a couple of nights a week.

When my father pointed out that my ex was bullying me and making it almost impossible for me to stay at the house with him, his mother said that it was all my fault, that I told lies and that it wasn't true. She told my father that my ex was a wonderful man and an exceptional father.

In hindsight, my feminist nerves get a little jangled here as I realise that I was only doing what he did. Yes, I was away a couple of nights a week, but so was he and yet it was acceptable for him – why not for me?

My parents were worried for me and felt that I should return home full time as they felt he was using this to get custody of our daughter.

They were right.

Unfortunately my escape had incurred yet another cost.

So why didn't I leave and **JUST** walk out?

The Devil and the Deep Blue Sea

He had got used to having the house without me in it. He did not want me there and was hell bent on letting me know that.

I went to the council and explained our situation. I told them that we could not live together a moment longer as it was making us all unwell. I told them that he refused to leave the house and that I was willing to sign the tenancy over to my ex.

The council officer asked if I could afford to buy or rent privately. I laughed and explained that I was unable to. The council officer made it clear that even if I did sign the house over to my ex, they couldn't rehouse me as it would mean I had chosen to make myself intentionally homeless.

Women's refuges have many women living there who, by removing themselves and their children from a toxic environment, are punished as they have made themselves intentionally homeless. They wait until they are fortunate enough to be rehoused, or they return home.

They said I would not get help renting privately either. When I asked why, they reminded me that I would have chosen to move out and therefore they would not help me.

The council advised me to stay in the house. They informed

me that my ex would be unable to keep it anyway because he was able to work and had a substantial amount of money that he had inherited from his father, which meant he could afford his own place. She did point out that if he had full custody of our daughter, however, then he would be given the place.

My psychological health deteriorated.

So why didn't I leave and **JUST** walk out?

Mental Health

I can't remember a time when I haven't been affected by my mental health. For many years I was plagued with agoraphobia, nightmares and flashbacks. Psychiatrists would meet me and try to explain what could have caused it. I knew something awful had happened when I was a child but I had forgotten it.

The past tortured me through these flashbacks and nightmares. Everything became distorted and twisted. Without my memories, anyone and anything could be a potential threat.

Sadly my ex-partner used this against me.

Even once I retrieved my memories of what had actually happened as a child, and established that the perpetrators had long since moved from the village I grew up in, he still used it to stop me being able to see my family. After all, how did I know that I wouldn't remember more? No, best to avoid anyone from my past!

My psychotherapist had seen through my ex and she tried her best to point out his inconsistency and how controlling he was, but unfortunately it was several years before I could see.

To Speak Or Not To Speak?

Whilst part of me would like to keep quiet and forget it happened, I can't. Not one single day goes by where I am not affected by my abusive past. I believe what happened to me was cruel and unjust.

My uncle died this morning. I loved him wholeheartedly. He was the bravest, coolest man I knew; all my cousins and I looked up to him.

My uncle met my daughter twice. He has died not knowing her, just like my poor grandparents. My daughter will never know what amazing people she has missed out on.

Today I am struggling to forgive myself for not standing up sooner. Today I have asked myself yet again, why didn't I **JUST** get out sooner? Why didn't I **JUST** fight harder?

QUESTIONS, QUESTIONS, QUESTIONS

Question: Do I regret leaving him?

Answer: Never.

Question: Do I regret going into a refuge?

Answer: Never.

Question: Do I regret not getting out sooner?

Answer: Absolutely.

Question: So why didn't I?

Over the last few years I have heard so many questions being asked of me or other women in my position . . .

Question: Why do you stay if it's so bad?

Question: Do you think perhaps you're exaggerating?

Question: Surely if you are so unhappy you would leave?

Question: You obviously love him, otherwise you wouldn't stay, right?

Question: Well he must be doing something right, you've been with him for over ten years haven't you?

Question: But he seems so nice, are you sure?

Question: But he is so handsome and charming. Isn't he?

Question: Do you think on some level you enjoy being treated badly?

I have asked myself these very same questions over the years and I never came up with one single answer whilst I was there, living with him. Removing myself from him has enabled me to finally find the answers I needed . . .

Question: So why didn't I **JUST** leave him?

Answer: For years it was because I believed that he loved me. Later, it was because I had no money, I had no confidence, I couldn't move back home as it was over a hundred miles away and I wasn't allowed to take my daughter with me.

Question: So why didn't I **JUST** put my daughter in the car and take her with me if he was so bad? What could he have done anyway?

Answer: He would have stopped at nothing to get my daughter back. He would have stooped to any level to ensure she didn't come with me.

Question: Why on earth did I stay so long?

Answer: I was waiting for him to see sense, see what he was not only doing to me and our daughter, but to himself, too. He was making himself as miserable as us.

Question: I knew he wouldn't take responsibility. He always believed he was right. Why didn't I get it?

Question: He will never, ever change, so why did I stay so long?

Question: So why did I stay so long?

Question: So why did I stay so long? . . .

Like a tuneless, colourless carousel, those words still repeat themselves over and over in my head.

BROKEN ANGELS

When I was advised to Google the term 'domestic abuse' I did so with some scepticism. Could I answer 'yes' to some of the questions it asked?

Before I knew it, I had pretty much answered yes to every question.

So there it was on the screen staring back at me, instructing me that I was indeed a victim of domestic abuse.

'That can't be right, surely?' I asked myself aloud and then decided to go back and reread it.

Not only was it right, but I'd managed to answer 'yes' to another question that I'd pretended not to read properly the first time round!

I told my two closest friends what I had discovered and they gave me strange, knowing looks, as if to say, 'Well yes of course you are, stupid.'

I was not, however, entirely convinced. I mean he'd never actually hit me – ever. And peppered amongst years of misery and madness were moments of love and happiness.

When my home environment became unbearable, I realised that I needed more support from somewhere. My daughter's wellbeing was being affected by it all by now and I knew it had to stop. I called the Domestic Abuse Helpline and left a message. Within hours a woman phoned me back. I liked her voice. There was something exceptional about it. She was as familiar with my story as though she had witnessed the entire thing. She offered comfort, just like Big Ted, my treasured teddy bear who had witnessed all my secrets and all my pain as a child. She understood exactly what I was going through. She was so confident that I had made the right call. This was what I had needed for so long.

She asked me lots of questions, similar to the ones that I had answered on the website. She then asked me if I could cope until the following Monday.

This was incredible, I mean I had coped alone all these years and here was someone finally giving a damn, who 'got' what I was going through.

I agreed to meet her and a colleague on the following Monday and that experience will remain with me forever. I can only describe it as like a light being switched on, illuminating the darkness of my sorry state, from the second I met her.

'I feel phony. I shouldn't be here, and, I mean, he has never hit me,' was my initial intuitive defensive response.

She of the calming voice pulled out a little card from her bag and told me to read it, whilst she bought me a reassuring cup of tea. On one side, written in green, was 'Mr Right', but on the other written boldly in red . . . 'Mr Wrong'.

A flimsy little card, thirty-eight short, sharp statements. It was more powerful than anything I had read in a long time.

She returns with the comforting cup of tea and the significant look we exchange bonds our thoughts and seals the next part of my journey. She knows she can help me . . . and I'm hooked!

DAY ONE

> All the past boyfriends are mocking me now.
> Watching and laughing and chanting somehow:
> 'You thought he'd be better,
> you thought he'd be kind.
> He's the worst of the lot and you're losing your mind.'

This is a strange place.

The walls seem to hold so many secrets, so much pain and fear, and yet there is the sense of this place urging you on, willing you to keep going. You must not give up, you must keep focused.

Women here have been so broken and bruised and yet their capacity to offer support is astounding.

The evidence of their pain, invisible but oh, so real, seems to be scattered around the house; you stumble upon it everywhere you tread.

Some of the women will appear to look you in the eye and yet look beyond you to a distant place where perhaps they keep themselves protected, tucked away and safe. I'd seen something similar in the eyes of my cherished cousin, a marine . . . I recall him coming to visit me a couple of years ago and I had been struck by the horror his eyes revealed. Some people can surprise you with their stories of pain and suffering, but his had been branded into his soul and now seeped through his eyes. Some of the women will return your glance and you may recognise something so intense and so uncomfortable that you feel the need to look away but you can't. They hold you captive with eyes that have witnessed more than a human being should ever have to see.

Having been accustomed to years of insult and blame and abuse, their ability to accept anything from another human being is humbling. A personal compliment, or the simple offer of a slice of bread to feed a child, means more to them than a diamond-encrusted bracelet given, perhaps, to another woman who has not been broken.

I think they would give you the clothes off their own back if they could, regardless of how much they may need them. These women have spent their lives giving all of themselves away to others, saving not one single piece for themselves.

These women, like broken angels, flee to this place of refuge. In an environment of peace and security they are able to mend their shattered bodies and heal their very hearts and souls, fragmented through years of torment and abuse.

Some carry their children with them. I call them the 'little angels'. They seem to relish all that is on offer in this brave new world.

Slowly you watch these broken angels become whole again, protected by the love and support of the unbroken angels who give their time to heal others.

During the journey to the refuge, my daughter asked if I was taking her to a mental hospital. I said, 'No, darling, why on earth would I need to do that?' I realised at that moment the extent of the fear her father has implanted in her poor little head about her 'crazy' mother.

Then she asked, 'Will the people be weird?'

I answered, 'I hope so, darling; weird can be wonderful. Perhaps they will find you and me weird.'

She quickly replied, 'Well I'm certainly not weird.'

Then she asked, a little more thoughtfully, 'Is it like a commune?'

I tried to change the subject but the questions were coming thick and fast; I needed to answer carefully.

My darling daughter was lost in thought for a few moments and then, suddenly appalled with the result, asked, 'Oh no, do we need to share bathrooms? Ugh, no! I bet they'll all have germs.'

'Of course there'll be germs; everyone has germs, darling, including us, but the house is spotlessly clean, I promise.'

So we are here . . .

Twenty-four hours later and we have settled into communal life, hidden away, secure from the world. This morning I started to realise what on earth I was doing here. What I was hoping to achieve. You see, until this morning I felt like some kind of imposter. How dare I intrude on this level of grief and pain when I was merely visiting with my daughter for a while?

This morning, whilst brushing my teeth, I took an honest look at myself for the first time in months. My eyes sparkled and my lips curved into a slight smile but then, as I maintained my gaze, reality dawned and I felt the weight of the blow as my knees trembled. I realised from the image in front of me that I, too, was one of the 'broken angels'. The pain of oh so many years of neglect and abuse revealed a face I could barely recognise and so I could look no more.

As I drove my daughter to school that morning, I understood that the full extent of my fear was sitting right beside me. This beautiful child was wearing that haunted look. Her eyes had already seen too much for her years.

So now it made sense.

She is the reason we are here.

She is the reason we escaped to the refuge, so that she will learn to recognise the signs of abuse. She will know that it is never acceptable for one person to treat another with such little thought, such little regard that their very spirit is broken and bowed.

We are here together, in my desperate quest that she will be able to grow and flourish and not become 'one of them'.

PETAL

A happy, smiling, little girl, skipping up to bed,
Teddy bears and pretty dolls, sleeping at your head.
You went away to stay one night, to learn a different game,
You went to stay away that night and never came home again

Once upon a time there was a pretty little blonde girl called
Petal. She was a dear little thing, always happy, always playing
with her dolls and teddy bears. She created a beautiful, peaceful
world for them all to play together in her bedroom.

Petal was such a kind little girl and loved her home so much.
She knew she was lucky to have a mummy and daddy who loved
her and she knew she had a beautiful home and that some
children weren't as fortunate as her.

Petal had a best friend called Snowdrop. Snowdrop was the
sweetest, kindest friend in the world. Petal and Snowdrop were
so close and loved playing with their dollies together. Some days
the girls' mummies would make them the most delicious picnics
and they would go off on their little bicycles and eat and chatter
together.

One day Petal met Rose and they soon became friends.

Petal and Snowdrop welcomed Rose into their friendship but
the dynamics didn't quite work. Rose was a tough girl and Petal
found her a little intimidating, and was unable to understand the
strange feeling she got in her tummy when she was around Rose.

Rose wasn't keen on Snowdrop so Petal began to see them
separately, but this became difficult as Rose was always
knocking on Petal's door and asking her to go out to play.

Petal felt very sorry for her new friend as she lived in a sad house. Petal felt guilty as she had a beautiful bedroom, fit for a princess, whilst poor Rose's bedroom had no pictures or mirrors, hardly any toys and hardly any books. Her friend had to share a bedroom with her little siblings and had no privacy.

Petal's mummy and daddy felt sorry for Rose, too, and let Petal spend lots of time at their house, feeding her and letting her stay over. Rose loved staying at Petal's house. She told Petal that she felt safe there.

Rose kept asking Petal to go to her house to play and to have tea. Petal wasn't keen, and neither was her mummy, but Petal didn't want to hurt her friend's feelings.

Petal went for tea a couple of times but couldn't wait to get home. Rose had a wicked stepfather who was horrible to her and her family, but Rose told Petal that her stepfather liked her.

Petal missed Snowdrop but she knew she had let Snowdrop down and that she hadn't been very nice to her. But Rose was always demanding so much of Petal's time and if Petal was honest with herself, she was actually quite frightened of Rose and was afraid to say no, so she would go for play dates.

Play days at Rose's house were very different to the days she spent with her other friends. Sindy, Barbie and Girls' World were nowhere in sight. Play days with Rose involved dressing up in grown-up clothes and underwear and swimsuits and having her photo taken by the stepfather and the two big brothers.

The stepfather had a Polaroid camera so the pictures were available instantly for them to look at. Petal was confused by the attention she received from this man and his stepsons but she liked to please people, and he was clearly pleased by her.

One day Petal agreed to a sleepover at Rose's. Petal was very nervous about staying away for the night as she wasn't used to having sleepovers. This sleepover proved to be quite something else!

She had been promised that the ogre wouldn't be there as he

drove a great big lorry around the country and was away a lot.

At the sleepover all was going well as they sat and ate their tea together. Then one of the brothers persuaded their mother to go with him to the off-licence to buy lots of cigarettes and alcohol.

Before she knew what was happening, Petal had tried the cigarettes and her head was spinning and her mouth tasted disgusting. She had wanted to look grown up in front of the big boys but she couldn't understand why anybody would want to smoke. As the evening wore on, her head grew more and more giddy and eventually she knew she had to go to bed.

She awoke to find one of the big brothers was in the top bunk bed with her and she was in pain so she screamed out. Her friend's mummy came into the room and scolded the boy.

Poor Petal was so scared she could not stop crying. She could not understand what was hurting so much.

The ogre came home unexpectedly and found Petal crying. Her friend's mummy was crying too. He was furious. He told Petal that if she dared tell her parents what had happened then he would kill her father and the little girl believed him because he was such a horrible man.

Petal kept begging to be taken home to her mummy and daddy but she agreed to stay as she felt so sorry for her friend's mummy. She had run the little girl a lovely warm bubble bath. As she sat beside her she sobbed and begged Petal never to tell her mummy or daddy about what had happened.

Petal reassured the mummy that she would never tell and, besides, she didn't really know what had happened anyway.

The next day Petal returned home and was enjoying playing a game with her dolls' house when her daddy called her downstairs. Her friend's mummy had cycled down to see her, so Petal ran outside to the gate where she stood to reassure her that she was fine and that she hadn't mentioned anything about last night to her parents.

Petal skipped back indoors and back to her dolls' house but was bemused for a second as she couldn't find Izzy, the little girl from the dolls' house family. She eventually found her stripped naked, shut in the wardrobe with wool tied around her mouth. 'How strange,' she thought, 'I don't remember doing that.'

Life changed dramatically for Petal after that.

She became terrified of the dark and found she was unable to sleep. She attempted to sleep in cupboards but developed claustrophobia so she began to sleep under beds with stacks of books and boxes in front of her so no-one could find her. She would pretend to feel sick, lock herself in the bathroom and attempt to sleep in the bath, but it was so cold.

She lived in a permanent state of high alert and constant stimulation. She could not cope. Over the next few weeks the little girl seemed to lose track of time and she kept losing things. Sometimes while at school she would fall asleep at her desk and be told off by the teachers. Sometimes she couldn't remember the simplest things like how to even dress herself.

Petal's school work suffered and her grades were slipping. She had been top of her class for each subject and was destined for the top set, but within the first few months of secondary school she dropped from top set to bottom. Not only were her grades plummeting but she was mixing with the wrong crowd. She was smoking and drinking when she could, she became spiteful and nasty and had started shoplifting. The girl despised who she had become and liked to punish herself.

Mummy decided it was time to do something about her daughter as she was so worried about her, so she was sent to a posh private school. Luckily it was an all-girls school and without the distraction of boys the little girl could concentrate on her studies.

When Petal entered her teenage years she found she

struggled with relationships. She did care about a friend of her brother but he seemed almost too nice to her and she didn't trust boys being nice.

As she grew up she couldn't understand why her life was such a mess when she'd had such a lovely, privileged childhood. She lived in a beautiful home with two parents who loved her and even had her own horse to enjoy, so why could she never hold down a job? Why were her relationships doomed to failure, picking one low-life loser after another? Why was she such a bad judge of character? Why was she so easily fooled by them?

This didn't seem to happen to her friends; they weren't involved with the type of boys she was. Her friends' boyfriends had proper jobs and took them to special places. Hers never had any money and if she was lucky she might have been taken to the pub of an evening to watch them play pool with their mates.

Why was she so terrified of the dark?

Little Petal had buried her memories so deep inside her that big, grown-up Petal couldn't find them anywhere.

She had conditioned herself to stay awake for years growing up and so needed something now to make her sleep. She found that alcohol was just the thing. Alcohol became her best friend. It was always there, it never let her down and it took all her fear away.

TED & PETAL

Too many Teds
So many Petals
Beautiful flowers
Strangled by nettles

As Petal grew into a woman she struggled.

She moved away from her hometown when she was eighteen and tried to find a new home but nowhere felt safe, nowhere felt like home.

Petal moved to London where she started having the most unusual turns. The ground would spin; she couldn't look up to the sky because it would make the ground spin even more. She would need to hold on to walls, or trees, anything that would prevent her falling over.

Petal lost every job she had.

She couldn't face people and so she cocooned herself at home.

Over the years Petal went from doctor to doctor, yet not one of them knew what was making her so ill. Eventually she was referred to a special doctor who asked her about her dizzy turns and her fears, which had become quite obsessional.

Petal was passed from counsellor to counsellor. Eventually someone realised that psychotherapy could be the answer.

Petal had some very strange habits and behavioural rituals and was told that by talking about them and understanding them, eventually they could stop affecting her.

Petal spent each and every week talking until she was blue in the face. She was determined to make herself better.

Petal went from one awful boyfriend to the next. Eventually

41

she found a nice boyfriend and they moved out of London and got married. At last Petal could start the life she had always dreamt of having. Alas, Petal let her husband down badly. Petal hated herself even more now for letting him down.

Petal was of a nervous disposition. She was clumsy and had very little confidence. Petal was renowned for stuttering and stammering and keeping herself confined within her safe little group of friends. Petal had an unusual job but one she adored with all her heart. She worked in a band where she wrote and performed songs.

One day Petal could not believe her luck when she met her knight in shining armour. His name was Ted and he was stunning. He looked like the hero from a 'Mills and Boon' novel. Tall, dark and handsome, he really did fit the description.

Ted vowed to protect Petal and her dear little dog forever. Ted said he loved dogs and that he loved going for long walks. This pleased Petal so much as Petal's dog meant more to her than anything.

Petal tingled and tickled in her tummy. At last, Ted had arrived. Petal smiled and dreamt of Christmas . . .

Petal loved those perfect Christmas cards that she would gaze at year after year, depicting the perfect, happy couple walking hand in hand through the woods with their dog trotting happily at their side. Petal would picture the couple returning to their happy home with a mantelshelf decorated with a Christmas garland and fairy lights framing the most beautiful roaring fire. The couple would sit beside one another and enjoy a glass of warm mulled wine, listening to Christmas songs.

Petal pinched herself hard. She couldn't believe she had found her dream. The fairytale really did exist after all.

It was a beautiful, new, budding relationship and one she had never experienced before. Ted was so handsome and so attentive. He would ask Petal lots and lots of questions about *her childhood. He would listen to the tales of pain she had been subjected to at the hands of others. Ted was furious.*

'How dare someone treat my beautiful princess so badly?'

Petal would say: 'It's fine, Ted; none of that matters now that I have you.'

Ted would lift her into his arms and spin her round and kiss her and make love to her over and over and over and over and over again.

To be told by this beautiful man that he would protect her meant more to Petal than anything, as she had never really been protected before. Well . . . maybe after a fashion, but you see Petal had learnt from a very young age that protection came at a very high price. But that was history now.

Oh how Ted loved his Petal! He couldn't keep his hands off her and she could not believe that such a perfect man would find her so attractive and want to be with her. 'Oh lucky, lucky me,' she would say and hug herself . . .

Day Three

Mummy and baby set off in the car
Mummy and baby don't get very far
Big, scary monsters are in hot pursuit
When Mummy's not looking they hide in the boot

Everyone has booked themselves out for the weekend, including us. Our bags are packed and ready to go. However, I've decided to wait until the rush-hour traffic calms down, and so I cook.

Wandering around the kitchen I reflect on how safe this place feels. Security cameras are positioned to protect us, the members of staff are here all day giving their time and support and never-ending patience. It matters to them that each and every one of us is OK. Whether it's a chat we need, help with the children or advice with sorting finances, there really isn't anything these incredible people won't help us with.

It feels strange but comforting to have my support worker come and find me each day to check on how I am feeling and how my daughter is coping. It wasn't until we had moved in here that I understood just how chaotic and abusive my life had been.

My daughter has made an enormous effort, considering that on our first night she announced she would not be leaving our bedroom and refused to talk to anyone.

I am overwhelmed by the way she has coped. I often well-up just looking at her these days. This morning I heard her giggling in the kitchen with a couple of the other women she has already become quite friendly with. The women here have gone out of their way to make us feel welcome and yet there's never any pressure to mix. If you choose your own space you'll get it, but if it's company you need it's there too: no pressure.

Cooking completed, I dish out our food and call my daughter down.

'Mummy . . .'

'Yes, darling,' I reply, with fork poised halfway between plate and mouth.

'I accidentally closed the bedroom door and the keys are in there!'

Panic grips me, but I try to sound calm as I realise our whole world is in that room. I call my outreach worker; thank goodness she has kept her phone switched on. She tells me she doesn't have a master key and that unless she can track the manager down, then my daughter and I will have to camp out on the sofa all weekend! She is joking of course. She calls back to tell me she's managed to reach the manager who had been on her way home, and that she was now on her way back with a master key.

About forty minutes later, our rescue is at hand. The refuge manager arrives wearing the most beautiful pair of Doc Martens. I notice my daughter checking them out too. She is drenched and laughing because she's just had a water fight with some of the teenagers from the other refuge house.

My daughter eyes the manager with suspicion, unsure of whether or not she will get told off for locking us out of our room and putting her to so much trouble on a Friday night.

I keep apologising over and over again until the manager stops laughing and looks me directly in the eye. 'You have said sorry. Once is enough; we only apologise once here!'

Trying to lighten the moment I say, 'So we aren't going to be evicted then?'

She bursts out laughing again and continues to tell my daughter all about the water fight. By the time the manager leaves I feel that she has done much more for us in that moment than just the practical application of key in lock. She had seen a mother and her daughter painfully uncomfortable in one another's company and she gently glued us back together with her humour and good sense.

I am sure she could feel the strain between us.

My poor, poor daughter looks so bewildered these days and I can't bear to see the look of uncertainty in her eyes. We'd become virtual strangers due to my absence and fear. I'd had to remove myself from the family home for so long. My psychotherapist had been as concerned as me about the effect all the arguments were having on my poor innocent daughter, so she had suggested that I removed myself to prevent things affecting her any more than they already had. I had taken her advice, but part of me regrets it now, as I sometimes feel the gap between us has grown so wide. Her father, I know, has made me look awful in her poor little eyes.

The manager gets up to leave. I want to cry out, 'Please don't leave us!' I don't, of course, but a big black cloud descends over my head. I wish I could take her with us both for the weekend.

What an amazing woman. She was an icebreaker for both of us which helped to unite us for the next few days.

. . . As one month merged into a second, Petal grew more and more in love with this beautiful man. She did find it slightly strange, however, that Ted never took her anywhere. When she mentioned it to him, he explained that they needed to get to know one another, as this was the mistake that most couples made. 'They just don't take the time to get to really know each other, Petal.'

When Petal said that her friends were missing her and that she was missing them, Ted said, 'Petal, darling, if they are real friends then they will be happy for you to go into the woods for a while with the man you love.'

Petal thought of the Christmas card again and smiled; she knew that Ted was right. Ted was always right and they made love again and again and over and over.

Petal was a daydreamer, she always had been and now she found herself often dreaming of nights out with her friends and Ted. She wanted to share this incredible man with them but, alas, even after several weeks of going into the woods with him, it still didn't seem to make a difference. Ted wasn't up for any of the things she tried to organise.

On Petal's birthday she desperately wanted to go out with her friends and Ted. Her best friend and their manager had gone to a big music conference in the South of France and were flying home early to spend her birthday with her. Petal told Ted of her plans and asked him if he would come. Ted, however, said that whilst he did want to spend her birthday with her, he would like to do so just the two of them.

Petal was bitterly disappointed and got a bit upset. Ted started getting sulky and it was making Petal nervous but she stuck to her guns. She hadn't seen her friends in days and they had been her life for so many years that she was desperate to see them.

Poor Ted looked so hurt that Petal called her manager back and tried to postpone the meal, but he explained that he was bringing with him a very special gift: a record deal.

Petal squealed and squealed her delight. She hung up the phone and grabbed Ted saying, 'We've got a record deal!'

Ted smiled but it didn't quite reach his beautiful eyes. He seemed to pull away and looked a bit grumpy. He said he was pleased for Petal, but something about his reaction contradicted what he said.

Petal felt a little deflated by the time Ted left.

Petal went out for dinner and tried so hard to enjoy the enormous effort her friends and management had made to make her birthday special. Petal never drank champagne as she never had any money, but her manager had bought her a large bottle back from France.

No-one had made so much effort for her before and she was so grateful, but she was preoccupied. She felt weird; she felt unsure and uncomfortable. She tried to work out why she felt sad when she was clearly so in love, but some strange niggle wouldn't let up.

Ted had promised to take Petal out for dinner for her birthday later in the week but didn't. Petal was disappointed and she was still frustrated that he hadn't come out to celebrate her birthday with her friends.

Eventually she plucked up the courage to complain to him that he never came anywhere with her or took her anywhere. Ted explained how his job as a musician meant long nights in pubs, clubs and venues, and when he had a night off he wanted to eat in quiet restaurants and rest at home and to be with Petal. Poor, poor Ted; he loved her so much and yet she was the dissatisfied one.

Petal decided to find a lovely restaurant to take him to but, alas, Ted didn't like the local restaurants. Ted said the types of restaurants he enjoyed were in France and that the French got it right but that England didn't.

When Petal said it made her sad that he never seemed to want to come out with her, Ted assured her that they could go on dates later, as it was important they bond sexually and emotionally first.

Petal realised that Ted was talking a lot of sense and it seemed silly to spend money on a restaurant if he wouldn't enjoy it.

So, Petal tried something else . . .

One of her long-cherished dreams was to go for long walks with Ted and that together they would take her dear little dog with them. Although Ted had said he loved walking when he first met her, what Petal hadn't realised was that Ted only liked walking in the countryside. Ted said that the walks local to them had too many people, too many dogs and too much dog poo.

Petal often questioned Ted's feelings for her little dog; even her best friend had pointed out that Ted didn't seem keen on dogs. Whilst Ted said he liked the dog, it was becoming clear that he didn't. This really worried Petal, as she loved her little dog and he seemed so unhappy these days and didn't wag his tail very often anymore.

Petal thought of the Christmas card again, but this time it just made her feel a little sad and uneasy.

Day Twenty-One

Baby's getting angry
She doesn't want to stay
Daddy's gone doolally
And Mummy's gonna pay

I go to visit my unbroken friends in their unbroken homes with their unbroken families, and the guilt flows thicker than black treacle in my veins.

My daughter has spent a few days with her father and has come back very different. She seldom catches my eye any more. Her father has crawled so far into her head that the poor child can't see straight.

He, of course, is the poor wounded hero and I am the evil one who only allows minimal contact and has chosen to move away from the 'happy home', dragging that poor child to the house of broken angels. She could have remained at home, a broken home but surrounded by the familiar, offering the only stability she has truly known since she was four years old. I think I could accept anger, tears or tantrums from her, in fact anything but this cold, indifferent numbness that has become my daughter.

We have a wonderful trip planned. I have the chance to take my daughter to a recording of one of her favourite TV shows and just for a few moments she forgets our miserable situation. She looks at me and smiles; I return the grin, hoping for some light-hearted mother-daughter chatter, but then nothing more is said. It's all gone again. She's remembered we live among the broken angels. The guard comes back up and it seems safer to be indifferent and numb.

. . . Within three months Petal was pregnant. Ted was delighted for Petal to carry his child. Petal was pleased but frightened. Her long-term anxiety disorder seemed to rear its ugly head with the fear of the unknown.

Petal was also worried, as she knew that her being pregnant would affect the lives of the people she was working with. Ted assured her that if they were real friends then they would be delighted for her and support her. If not, then it was best to find out now.

Everyone who Petal was working with, from the band members to the record company guys, was determined to work around the pregnancy so Petal felt reassured and happy. Ted was not happy.

Over the next few weeks, Ted said that her band was being disrespectful and resentful towards him. Petal could not understand this as each and every time she and Ted met her friends they always seemed polite. In fact, round this time she was house sharing with of one the guitarists who was her best friend, and he had allowed Ted to stay there too, rent free, for the best part of two months.

Petal came to the conclusion that her friends must be being horrible to Ted when she wasn't looking. She knew that Ted would never lie. He had made her a promise and he was so appalled by the way others had treated her that she knew Ted was telling the truth. No, she clearly had not known these friends as well as she thought, even though she had been close to them for the best part of ten years. Ted was clearly a much better judge of character than her.

On the rare occasion that Ted would take Petal to the pub, it always resulted in Petal upsetting poor Ted. If she spoke to her friends at the bar Ted would accuse her of talking about him, saying that her friends looked at him funny. He accused Petal of wanting to keep her friends separate from Ted. When she argued that it was untrue and reminded him how she had tried getting him to come out with them all several times, he would tell her that she enjoyed the divide. This baffled Petal as she really didn't see that this was what she was doing, although Ted was probably right, as Ted was always right and, besides, her hormones were all over the place.

DAY THIRTY-ONE

A little glimpse of normal
Amongst the broken home
A little piece of comfort
Whilst standing all alone

Thank heavens the indifference subsided for a while to allow my daughter to snap and throw a complete hissy fit.

Of course, I didn't want to see her upset, but to see her become rude and obnoxious was a welcome relief. Her emotions were finally released from the tight rein she had been holding on them. The breakthrough did not occur at the refuge but in the familiarity of a friend's home, over something as simple as asking her to take a shower.

Daughter snapped, daughter screamed, 'So were you ever forced to take showers at friends' houses?!' Daughter slams the door and I burst into tears.

In that private moment, whilst driving away from my friend's, I chose to do the 'Talk of Truth' with my daughter that the unbroken angels had persuaded me was unavoidable. They had made me realise that whilst it was admirable that I refused to bad-mouth my daughter's father, it meant she only had one side of the story, and whilst she didn't need to hear all the gory details, she did, however, need to be told the truth.

'I'm sorry I got upset, darling, but you were rude and I don't deserve that.'

She denies being rude but I don't back down. I continue, 'Do you really think I want to "borrow" friends' showers? Do you really think I want to live in a refuge?'

I pause just long enough in the hope that it will add power to the message.

'Listen, darling, I feel very embarrassed that we have to use friends' houses in order to keep in touch with the people we care about. I'm sorry we have to stay with friends at the weekend but you know we can't have visitors at the refuge, don't you? My friends are doing the best they can to help us and it isn't ideal for them either, but do you know what? Everyone is trying their best to do all they can to help you and me.'

Then came the hard bit.

'I'm sorry if you're feeling angry and upset about what is happening right now. I understand you miss home; I want to go home, too, darling, but I can't. Daddy is there and to go home is to say it's OK for Daddy to treat me as he has and, you know what, it isn't OK. Do you understand that? To take you back there is to say to you that it's OK for someone to treat someone else with disrespect and this is *so* not OK! Do you understand?'

I know she's panicking and I feel terrible that perhaps I've said too much, but the truth needed to be told. I turn and look at her.

'I love you, sweetheart, and I'm sorry you're hurting and unsettled but I will never allow anyone to treat me this badly again. You lived in the house, my angel, surely you must know that Daddy wasn't very nice to Mummy? I want you to learn the truth so that you will never have to suffer as I have. I could not look you in the eye if you didn't learn these harsh lessons. Do you understand, darling?'

I sit and contemplate. I question for probably the billionth time, should I just go back home with her? Could I take just a few more years? Just until she goes to college or university?

The journey and the talk over, I drop her off at another friend's house so she can see her best friend. I'm worried sick about her; she is so subdued and tired, but there is a tiny flicker behind the eyes that I have not seen in years. Did I see a little respect growing there? It's not a lot, but it's a start!

. . . Petal and her band launched their album of songs when she was eight weeks pregnant and Ted had insisted on driving Petal to the show in London Town. She had longed to travel in the big truck with the others; travelling with her band had always been so much fun.

For Petal, being in her band was the only time she truly relaxed. She was too shy to perform and so had created an alter ego to carry her through the performance and it was always such a release. But things were changing now for Petal and not only to her body.

DAY THIRTY-TWO

I want to move to Cornwall
and live beside the sea
I want to join a Shanty Band
to be what's left of me

Today is hard.

Today is Thursday.

I want to be in Cornwall. I want to be wandering around Looe, looking forward to tonight because tonight is sea-shanty night at the Jolly Sailor. I close my eyes and pretend I'm there, not here.

Today I am sitting with my solicitor.

My ex-partner has insisted that I have an alcohol test to prove I am an alcoholic and an unfit mother. Because I have a needle phobia, I am relieved when my solicitor tells me that a hair-strand test is far more accurate than a blood or urine test.

We both sit in silence for a while, waiting for the 'taker of my hair' to arrive. I watch my solicitor typing. She is so strong.

The last time I came to see her I brought along a friend as I couldn't drive myself. Panic attacks had taken over and I knew I wasn't safe to be driving.

I recall my solicitor's face that day. She had seemed so angry and I assumed it was with me, but I was wrong. She told me that she had sought a second opinion about my ex-partner, how she had spent some time going over the whole case with her colleague.

'My colleague and I have tried to understand his angle. Everybody has an angle and we've found only one.'

She paused then and looked from me to my friend, the long pause adding dramatic effect, before her next words cut to my core.

'The only angle we can come up with is that he is out to destroy you, nothing less.'

My entire body went cold and was covered in goosebumps; the fair hairs on my arms were standing up on end. I looked like a plucked chicken!

It was quite something to be told that by a solicitor who has pretty much heard it all, but to see shock, disgust, even sorrow on her face had got to me, frightened me, and warned me that he really would stop at nothing.

And now here I sit, watching her typing. She apologises and explains that she can't stop as she is busy working on another case, but needs to be here to witness my hair test.

There is a knock on the door and her secretary announces they are here. An enthusiastic graduate arrives who is full of excitement as she announces in her happy sing-song voice that I am only the second person on whom she has carried out the procedure. She gives me a form to fill in which asks about my alcohol and drug use. I tell her I do not take drugs but she smiles at me patronisingly as if to say, 'There's no smoke without fire.'

She asks my solicitor to sign, to vouch that she knows me and that I am indeed the person named on the form. My solicitor is polite; after all, the poor young girl is only doing her job, but perhaps my solicitor is thinking the same as me: does she really need to be enjoying her job as much as she is clearly showing?

The girl explains the procedure, tells me it will hurt a bit and that I will be left with a bald patch the size of a five pence coin. She promises to take it where it hopefully won't be seen.

It takes her a few moments to locate the area. I stare at my solicitor and just for a moment she stops typing and looks at me. I tell her, 'How weird, it's only a bit of hair and yet I have never felt so humiliated in my entire life; I am so embarrassed.'

She stares and takes a huge breath in. Just for a moment I can see a film of tears in her eyes, then she frowns, clears her throat and gets back to her typing.

'Ouch, that hurt,' I say as the hair is ripped out from my scalp.

'There, all done,' the girl announces excitedly.

I switch off now, rubbing my little bald patch as she chatters to my solicitor about where her next appointment is. She tells us that the results won't take long.

I get up to go, but my solicitor asks me to stay for a minute. We watch the graduate leave with my lock of hair safely sealed inside a sterile envelope.

My solicitor is looking at me again; it's more bad news, I can tell.

'Legal Aid has refused to grant you any funds. I heard from them this morning and it appears that your ex-partner has informed them that you own a piece of land which is worth a substantial amount of money. Unfortunately we cannot act on your behalf until they have looked into it.'

'The land is worthless; it will never be granted planning permission. It was given to me and my brother by my father but it's worthless; he just didn't want the worry of it.'

'You will need to get it valued and sent to the Legal Aid agency, but I must warn you that this could put the case back months.'

'Why on earth would he do this?' I ask, confused.

She looks at me as if I'm from another planet . . . 'I imagine it's to hold things up.' She looks like she wants to add the word 'stupid' to it, but I know she's far too polite.

'Well, I guess, but I don't see why.'

My solicitor looks at me as though I'm simple and speaks to me slowly: 'You were given a council house because you were classed as vulnerable by the council due to your anxiety disorder. You chose to put his name on the tenancy, which makes you joint tenants. The council have told you that they will not rehouse you. The person who gets custody of your daughter will get the house. His solicitor will have explained this to him so he needs to make sure he gets your daughter taken from you so that he can keep the house.'

I sigh as I remember a conversation I'd had with his mother not long ago. She'd looked me directly in the eyes and said, 'There is no way he will give up the house.'

'I'm sure he wouldn't do that to me and my daughter. He knows I have no more options. He's made it impossible for me to move her home to my parents and he knows I have no money,' I say baffled.

My solicitor looks irritable now and glares at me.

'He has just made you have an alcohol test to prove you are an unfit mother and all in his quest to get your daughter taken away from you; surely you aren't surprised?'

I guess, when she puts it like that, I must be pretty naïve to be surprised.

. . . The trip to London Town would only take forty minutes and Petal had promised everyone she would be there on time for the set-up and sound check. Petal swore that she and Ted would leave by 5pm to give them plenty of time to get there. Ted, however, had other ideas and decided he needed to buy some new clothes.

'But Ted, please, we need to leave, we can't let them down,' cried Petal.

Ted was furious and his language was atrocious. He told her in no uncertain terms that he would not rush about for them; that she was the important one in the band and that the others were dispensable.

'But Ted, I said I would meet you up there. I said I would go in the van.'

Ted was grinding his teeth and was red in the face. Petal didn't like it when he did this as it made him look mean and not at all handsome.

Poor Petal was beside herself with panic. To make matters worse, Ted insisted that she went with him to help choose something to wear.

'But Ted, I'm supposed to be getting my hair and make-up done for the show and I'm meeting the lady who's bringing my clothes – they may need altering – and, oh Ted, please hurry.'

'You do realise that I have turned down appearing on a TV show to be at your gig tonight. Do you know how much that has cost me? In a minute, Petal, I'll not go. You clearly don't want me there.'

'Oh, Ted, that's not true, of course I want you there,' exclaimed Petal. 'I just, I-I-I j-j-just . . . oh d'you know what, Ted, you're right! Forget them. Come on, let's go and choose your clothes and if we're late, well, I mean, they can hardly go on without me, can they?'

Ted wrapped her in his arms and told her over and over again how much he loved her. Ted was so happy now as they walked hand in hand to the shops.

Petal eventually arrived for the show an hour and forty minutes late. All the other band members were furious with her but, as bad and embarrassed as she felt, she was relieved because Ted was no longer sulking, so all was good again.

The album launch went well, but the band weren't happy with Petal and she knew in her heart that she had let them all down.

Ted shadowed Petal's movements the entire evening and kept hugging her, stroking her and kissing her, which Petal found peculiar as Ted had told her off once when she had tried kissing him in public. He had said in no way was that acceptable as he didn't like public shows of affection. He had clearly changed his mind and kept proudly placing his big hand over Petal's stomach, smiling into her eyes at their unborn child growing inside her.

Petal beamed with delight at everyone who came to speak to her and she introduced Ted to them all. He was charming and lovely to everyone. Lucky, lucky me, thought Petal.

After the album launch, the band's record company had managed to get them a deal in Japan. All was being checked by lawyers and if it went ahead it could mean the band were well on their way to success.

Ted was worried . . .

Ted went everywhere with Petal to protect his unborn child.

The rest of the band was getting fed up with Ted, and poor Petal felt helpless.

DAY FORTY-THREE

A wicked witch
Tatty jeans
A despicable man
Shattered dreams

I met with the social worker again today.

She looks at me with disgust and I'm not sure why. She had been reasonably polite the first time I had met her.

My solicitor's words of warning came back to bite me as I realised that perhaps she was right, my ex had upped the stakes to discredit me.

My key worker and I go to the quiet room with her and she soon makes it clear that she has no patience for me. She says her only concern is for the child and that as parents we should have been able to sort things amicably.

I try reassuring her that I did indeed try to sort things amicably through mediation and a few attempts at counselling and had tried for years, but she just looks at me as though I was dirt on her shoe. I realise she isn't listening so I sit in silence for a while.

The social worker tells me that after her initial brief meeting with me, she had spent a considerable amount of time with my daughter and her father at the family home. She then calmly and coldly announces that she has decided to recommend my daughter lives with her father there. She tells me that she has already let him know she thinks my daughter is better off with him.

I'm not sure what happened next as I think I zoned out. I must have asked why. I remember there were tears.

'To be honest, he presented himself as the far better parent,' I hear the social worker say.

'But how can that be?' I ask, confused by her statement.

'He had lots of medical evidence to back up his argument that your mental health issues prevent you from caring sufficiently for your daughter. He told me that you are unable to prioritise your daughter's needs over your own.'

The social worker glares at me then, as though I am scum. Funny that, I reflected, that was his name for me: scum. I was scum because I did not want to be with him any longer. I refused to live another day in the same house as him and I refused to subject my daughter to another day in that suffocating atmosphere.

I drew on what little strength I had left in me to argue. 'The medical evidence you say he has are my old, confidential psychotherapy notes from over ten years ago. Did you actually read them?'

She glares at me again. 'I don't have time to read everything, I have far more high-profile cases I need to deal with and I don't have time to siphon through his statements and yours. This report must be ready in a couple of weeks.'

I am completely stunned at this and I am aware that my support worker is also.

'But have you read my current medical notes that my solicitor sent to you?' I retort, trying to understand the social worker's thinking.

'No, as I said, I haven't got the time,' replies the social worker. 'You don't seem to understand, he has bombarded me with phone calls and paperwork arguing his case. He has sent statements written by his mother, aunt and sister and you don't look good in any of them. I had to end a call with him the other day, as he was ringing continually and leaving messages. I'm too busy and he exhausted me.'

I could not believe what I was hearing. So this woman, a trained social worker who is meant to be acting for the welfare of my poor innocent daughter, has decided that due to my ex-partner's bullying and continual onslaught on her, that my daughter is better off living with this man! I could not help but laugh. She had only experienced a few hours of his bullying and pestering whilst I have endured years of it, and she had fallen at the first hurdle.

'So let me get this clear. You have decided to recommend that my daughter lives with her father because he presented himself in a better light than me?'

She looks at me defiantly and proudly and answers, 'Yes.'

I continue to question her reasoning. I ask her to elaborate, please, and she tells me that when she visited my daughter and him in the family home she had found it spotlessly clean and orderly.

This bit of the conversation particularly makes me laugh as my best friend walks past the house each and every day, reporting back on how disgusting it looks, how the grass is overgrown and the windows all look filthy. She reported a couple of weeks ago, however, that she had seen his mother's car parked outside the house and that the lawn was all tidy and cut and the windows looked clean. I realised now that it all made sense; he was always one step ahead of me.

I sit and shake my head, I mean, look at me, I'm a mess. Look at the state of me in my ripped jeans, greasy hair and the words stuttering from my lips as I can hardly string a sentence together. I could picture him now. He's handsome and charming, and I'm not at all surprised she has chosen him.

The social worker is still talking and explains that he had

informed her that he had always done our daughter's homework with her, attended to her medical needs and that I had been too drunk and absent to be able to care for my daughter.

I challenged her.

'But this man would go away on tour with different bands, leaving me to look after our daughter. He was never concerned for her welfare because he knew she is safer with me than anybody. Oh, and I don't actually have a drink problem, unless a couple of glasses of wine an evening is a problem?'

She glares at me again, this time at the tears in my jeans. I nervously try to pull the pieces of fabric over my knees, cursing myself for not trying to find a better pair, and continue my defence.

'He subjected me to a humiliating alcohol test which proved I do not have any kind of drink problem whatsoever. He also subjected me to degrading psychiatric assessments which confirmed I am a perfectly fit mother. Did you see those results?' I ask.

I fumble on my scalp for my little bald patch. It has now got soft little bristles growing back and I've become quite obsessed with playing with it. I realise that soon it will have grown again and I shall miss it.

'No, I'm too busy; you don't understand, I have piles and piles of paper from him.'

Now she's getting really agitated, but I can't let this go.

'Had you read my current medical notes you would have also realised that I no longer have a mental health issue which, incidentally, was diagnosed as extreme anxiety. I was discharged from any support from the mental health team over four years ago. If you had read the letters my doctor has written, you would have also seen that she is more than happy with me and my skills as a mother.'

The social worker starts repeating herself: 'But the child needs to be settled and he does do all her homework with her. Is that correct?'

'Well, academically I'm not the sharpest tool in the box so, yes, he does sit with our daughter every evening and help her do her homework, so I can't really argue with that,' I concede.

I'm starting to flag now, my limited energies draining away. This was a social worker. Such professionals are responsible for making decisions on a child's future. This one had clearly decided that my daughter belonged with her father. I felt a floating sensation. It wasn't that I no longer cared, but it took me back to a horrible car accident I had been in.

I had been driving on the M1 when a van cut in front of me. I had braked and I remember the car had spun. I fought and fought with all my might but as I saw the central reservation heading towards me, in a surreal, slow-motion effect, I closed my eyes and let go of the wheel. I realised there was no more I could do. Here was that feeling again. I was letting go now. I closed my eyes and switched off.

I came back to the glorious sound of my support worker fighting on my behalf.

'But this woman was not allowed to help with the homework. This is what it is like living with an abusive partner; they control everything. He didn't allow her to do anything. This woman wasn't allowed to make any decisions without running them past him for his approval. This man limited her time so much that she wasn't allowed to read to her daughter for more than ten minutes before he insisted she leave her daughter to go to sleep. This man dictated where she should take her daughter and what she should feed her when he wasn't around at the weekend.'

I remember smiling at my beautiful support worker. She is young and so pretty and positive, but even she looks worried today.

The social worker asks me to go and get my daughter and I

dumbly obey. I walk her back to the quiet room and then escape to the lounge to cry. Immediately all the other broken angels gather to offer support, each and every one of them offering genuine understanding and affection. Thank heavens no-one hugged me or touched me. The broken angels here, like me, seem to be terrified of being touched.

'The social worker thinks he's a better parent, that I'm not good enough,' I wail. A couple of angels have tears in their eyes for me.

Eventually my daughter comes to find me and asks me to go back to the quiet room.

As I enter the room, the social worker glares at my exposed knees; again, instinctively I slouch a couple of inches, desperate to hide my knees and hoping that today isn't one of the days I've chosen to draw a smiley face on either one.

'You must thank your daughter, because she has asked to spend equal time with you both. I did recommend she stay with her father during the week to concentrate on her homework, and with you at the weekend, but she was adamant that she wishes to spend equal time with you both on a rolling three-day rota, so I will put that in the report.'

Job done, she stares at me with indifference now. I glare back.

'Thank your lucky stars that your daughter has chosen this way and, in future, I recommend that you're very careful about with whom you share details of your mental health!'

She leaves and I want to be sick, but just dry retch. My support worker was amazing, but she is appalled at what we had both endured. She will stand by me and help me should I wish to complain.

To be told by a social worker that you are an unfit mother is quite possibly the most horrendous label to be given. I wanted to give up, but thank God for my support network who gathered me up and got furious on my behalf.

My solicitor wrote a challenging letter to the social services, accompanied by copies of my current medical notes and alcohol test results. She also requested that the social worker in question attend the final hearing to justify her findings. She strongly urged the social worker to read the notes first as it was clear she was going on the notes from my ex-partner and certainly not authentic medical reports.

My support worker spoke to the refuge managers who also said they would stand by me if I chose to complain.

I visited my GP who, as always, gave me the strength to keep going. 'We have the proof that you are a lovely mum.' Her beautiful smile and her belief in me rubbed off that day.

It has to be said my gut reaction was to put my head down and stay quiet, but I couldn't help thinking that there seemed to be too many other people being neglected in this way, having their lives destroyed due to the negligence of the system. I had to make a stand. I mean, what if I hadn't been in a refuge? What if my support worker hadn't been present? I may not have had anyone to fight for me after I chose to give up.

. . . *During the pregnancy Petal watched helplessly as the members of her band and her friends deserted her. Ted said it was their loss and that they were not true friends. Secretly Petal was heartbroken. She knew that they had been left no choice as Ted was always present and he had an air about him which seemed intimidating and slightly menacing.*

Petal's hormones were making her feel quite unwell and she had no fight left in her, she had to stand by Ted; after all, he was the father of her unborn child.

By the time Petal was about to give birth, her band and her career had all gone. Ted told Petal not to worry about her music career, because with his contacts in the music industry he would find her a new band. Petal kept this new promise tightly in her heart with all the other promises Ted had made her. She used all of his promises to feed and water the love she felt for her wonderful man, believing that Ted would never lie to her.

Petal went into labour on her due date. After a long and difficult labour, Ted wandered around the delivery room bouncing their beautiful new baby they had named Bluebell, telling her over and over again how much he loved her.

Petal haemorrhaged badly and the doctor warned that she may need a blood transfusion, which terrified Petal.

The hospital gave Ted and Petal their own room so that Ted didn't need to leave Petal's side. Poor Ted grumbled at how uncomfortable the put-up bed was but soon drifted off into a deep sleep.

The day after their beautiful baby was born, Petal's parents had been on their way to visit them all in hospital. They had driven miles and miles to see her but Ted found out and telephoned them, telling them that if they came anywhere near the hospital then he would call the police. Heartbroken and bewildered, they had turned around and gone home.

Petal was devastated; she had so needed to see her mum and dad more than anything in the world.

Petal spent the next few days in hospital recovering her strength while Ted's parents came in and fussed over little baby Bluebell.

She watched as Ted overwhelmed their daughter, taking her from Petal's arms as soon as she finished breastfeeding, priding himself on doing everything for the child.

Ted no longer gazed into Petal's eyes, declaring his undying love. From the second baby Bluebell left Petal's body, so did Ted's obsessional love leave too. Ted had transferred all of his affection for Petal onto beautiful Bluebell.

Petal lay in her hospital bed feeling like a sterile incubator.

She kept longing to hold Bluebell and spend time just the two of them, but no sooner was the little girl awake than Ted was there beside the cot, reassuring her: 'It's alright Bluebell, Daddy's here, Daddy's here . . .'

Poor Ted was exhausted. He had been back to their home only to find that their poor little dog had been left too long and had gone to the toilet several times all over the brand-new carpets that Petal's parents had kindly bought for them. Petal tried soothing him but Ted was furious.

Ted said that he needed to get Bluebell home as his poor neck and back were killing him. Petal argued that she would be fine to look after Bluebell on her own if Ted wanted to go on home. But Ted reassured her that he must stay, as poor Petal had lost too much blood and needed to rest.

Whenever Ted's family came into the hospital to visit he would let them know how exhausted he was, how he was taking care of most of Bluebell's needs, except feeding her of course; Petal was doing that bit and very well!

Ted's mother would praise Ted for how wonderful he was tending to Bluebell and she would laugh at how the nurses all behaved around Ted. The nurses all clearly had a soft spot for Ted, as he was so very handsome and such a hero with his daughter. His mother, after finding the whole thing hilarious, would look at Petal and say, 'Oh take no notice, Petal; Ted only has eyes for you.'

Petal was momentarily stunned as she realised how little she cared.

Petal lay in bed feeling sore, frightened and alone. She desperately wanted to go home to her parents and spend a few weeks with them recuperating. She would sob her heart out. Ted made sure she didn't call her parents. She knew they would be heartbroken at being sent away, not allowed to see their granddaughter.

Petal realised that she was beginning to dislike Ted. She was beginning to find him a bit of an annoying know-it-all who absolutely loved himself, particularly the sound of his own voice.

Petal thought that this must be the aftershock of childbirth and it must be the hormones talking and certainly nothing Ted was doing wrong . . . surely?

Day Forty-Six

Legends in the making
Rock stars in disguise
Wizards of true meaning
Right before my eyes

I met with the refuge managers this morning at the 'other house'. My support worker had told them all about the social worker. They know that I've taken a huge nosedive emotionally since that bruising encounter. My confidence was already in tatters.

I knocked on the door and asked if I could talk to them. What an incredible force they are. I tried to find within me another experience that had affected me as much as these two women did . . . The most recent memory was when I once stood watching wolves in a zoo at twilight. It was a mystical experience that tingled through the pores of my skin and then through to my very core. These women had the same effect on me. You vow to treasure such an experience, to protect and hold it within you forever. You know it's a special gift and it's something that you can take out and hold if ever you should need to. I decide to store it, safely inside me in its own little drawer because it was so precious.

See, that's the problem once you are broken. You can become paranoid and you feel you should hide yourself just in case someone sees!

There are 'dark forces' who seek you out. These dark forces can spot you, it's like they have some invisible radar that tunes in to victims of domestic abuse. The dark forces don't reveal themselves at first; that would be just careless of them. No, at first they will appear loving, kind and protective. They will display genuine concern when you reveal the mistreatment you have suffered by the previous dark forces.

Then they inform you that if you would only just belong to them then they would never treat you 'in that way'. If only you could look closer, move beyond the sweet words and observe their minds tick, tick, ticking overtime, storing up all the little signs of your past abuse. Getting twitchy by your pain. Recalling your abuse is tantalising and titillating; you see this really gets them going!

At first they take little bites out of you, your money or your confidence. Then they may make you doubt yourself, your clothes, your abilities as a mother or your ability to clean, your cooking, your intelligence, even your career.

They will be oh, so subtle to start with, but they will be there, lurking like a stealth bomber waiting to sneak up on you. Who knows when it appeared but soon you feel the oppressive black shadow of the dark forces as it hovers above you.

It may not be long before they try to come between you and your friends, your family and, unforgivably, your own children.

Close your eyes for just a moment and picture a beautiful butterfly. Now see it being thrown to the ground and a big, heavy boot coming down on top of it, grinding and rolling it into the pavement until there is nothing left but a smudged stain.

I arrived at this moment in my life, a crossroad that generations have often spoken about. You have a choice to make. If you are lucky enough to still have heart and spirit you may make the right choice. An unbroken angel may seek you out and fly you to their sanctuary where they will heal all the little ouches first. Once these have gone they will mend the deeper hurt and lift your spirits until, one day, if you are lucky, your wings may repair and you will be free to fly again.

If you retreat from the crossroad you may be helped back home with the dark force, grateful to be simply stuck on their boot. There you may be given a little respite before the game starts up again. Have you ever watched a cat toying with a mouse? That's how it feels a lot of the time. They don't want to eat you. I'm not convinced they always want to kill you but I do know that they love the game.

Perhaps you are left on the pavement. Along comes another dark force. They scrape you off the ground and take you home to finish you off altogether.

Your remaining wish may be to lie smudged on the pavement, playing dead and praying for the rain to wash you away forever.

I imagine all the broken angels have learnt to section themselves off into safe little pieces but I realised that the two women I met with this morning in the refuge knew exactly where to find these pieces. The women bounce off each other like a comedy duo, but combine that humour with strength and wisdom and kindness. It is nothing short of awe inspiring.

Today I understood why men and women follow their leaders into battle. I would follow those two women anywhere.

I tell them the truth. The truth being that I was close to giving up, that he had pushed me one step too far, and that I had nothing left in me. I tell them that I had packed the few precious belongings I have of my daughter and was going to take them home and leave them there so when she returns from her holiday she will have them.

I tell them I want to disappear. Move to Cornwall and start a new life. Reinvent myself and sing sea shanties with the locals at the Jolly Sailor. We laugh about this.

Of course, they've heard it all before, I can see that as we enjoy a rare moment of bleak humour. But the atmosphere changed as they wondered just how serious my plans were.

Of course, I knew as soon as the words left my mouth that I could never do this. I could never give up on my daughter, not while there is breath in my lungs.

These wonderful women then gave me a rare glimpse into their own lives. They, too, have days when they feel like they've had enough, when they find it difficult to cope and just want to pack it all in. Although their work is stressful, they convince me that the pain and hardship I am going through is so much larger than their own and they praise me for my unbelievable strength.

I looked at them both closely; were they laughing at me or patronising me?

A tingling sensation shoots up one side of my body and back down the other side as I realise that they are sincere in their belief. They saw a strong, brave and wonderful mother.

I was the strong one.

We reminisce about the last few weeks that my daughter and I have lived in the refuge. They remind me of how my daughter was when we first arrived. Of the scared little girl who carried around her 'comfort blanket', which these days was a little bottle of antibacterial fluid, desperate to protect herself from the many germs her father had told her would seep into her pores and poison her whilst she lived at the refuge. The little girl who had announced that she would stay in our room and speak to no-one.

We smiled and chatted about the change in my beautiful daughter now. How she has taken to refuge life, how she now mixes with everyone and has embraced every aspect of communal living. They remind me of the gift I have given to her in the hope that she will recognise right from wrong and become empowered and confident in her life choices.

I leave the 'other house' feeling light hearted and walk to my car with a slightly cocky swagger. I jump in the car, choose my mantra song, 'Butterflies and Hurricanes', the song that I play on a loop these days, in desperate hope that its words and strength will get me through another day. I turn it up so loud that it starts to distort and I scream out the words.

I smile like I'm happy. Then my smile widens as I know I actually am happy. I'm not pretending this time.

As I drive through the traffic I wonder if the other vehicles may be carrying 'dark forces' out on the hunt for their next victim. I tingle in the knowledge that I am safe in the little bubble these women have placed around me.

But slowly my sense of well-being evaporates. Goosebumps prickle uncomfortably up my spine. I stop smiling and switch off the stereo and my thoughts are for all the other broken angels who never make it. Their lives and very souls punished and hurt on a daily basis.

I look suspiciously at the hundreds of cars which might be carrying the dark forces home. That's the problem with dark forces; they can lie hidden in the mundane and every day, disguised as decent human beings. Oh, we have all heard of the stereotypes, but what the refuge has taught me is that there is no 'type' when it comes to domestic abusers or their victims. Domestic abuse can touch anybody and cares nothing for hair or skin colour, financial situation or intelligence levels. They are mothers, fathers, husbands and wives, siblings, friends or partners. Anyone can be an abuser, anyone can be a victim.

I stare at a man who pulls up beside me. Was he a dark force driving home to his own broken angel? And was his angel wondering at this exact moment what the dark force would do when he returned home?

The poor man stares at me confused. I realise I've been glaring at him. My cheeks colour and then, as if by magic, the lights change and I can drive off.

I cannot shake off the idea of his guilt. What will he find wrong today? Will it be her clothes, the house, her attitude, the children, the dog or the cat? Anything or all of them, but definitely something will be wrong, something will need to be trampled upon or corrected, and someone will most certainly need to be punished.

I cried at that moment for all the children who were not enjoying their school holidays, who would also be wondering what will happen today. These children have such acute senses for their age. They have learnt to analyse every single sound, preparing them for what may happen next. If they're lucky then it may just be the clothes, the food, the house, the attitude, the dog or the cat, and it will be their mother who must be punished, not them.

The children may wonder if they can find the strength to stand up for their mother and stop the physical and emotional pain from being inflicted once again. They may think it better to take on the punishment themselves than to watch their mother take one more emotional or physical beating.

The children know, however, that one day they, too, will be wrong and will need sorting out without delay. Who knows, maybe this time it will be all of them?

The dark force will have completed its mission and had the last word.

There will be silence!

Children who survive this toxic environment may learn from their experience. Others, sadly, may grow to repeat the patterns of abuse and abuser. Blame may hang over their young lives as they were unable to stop the dark force from carrying out the particular brand of torture they endured. But how on earth could they? They were too small, they were only children.

I often question whether domestic abuse is infiltrated into our very beings as children. Surely no man or woman who grew up in a peaceful, loving environment could fall onto such an empty path? A journey without end, where no trees or flowers grow. The monotony of a grey, concrete walkway leading onward through the lifeless desert. Nothing on the horizon for the eye to see or to nourish the soul.

. . . When Petal and Bluebell were able to return home nobody visited except Ted's mother. She was lovely and brought over delicious meals and took their washing and ironing away with her.

Each day she would leave and Petal would sneak off to cry. Part of her wanted to beg Ted's mother to take her and Bluebell home with her. Petal adored her beautiful baby girl but was struggling with Ted.

Secretly she hadn't been able to get over Ted hurting her mum and dad. She had received a package of gifts and cards from her parents. It broke her heart.

Ted got angry.

Petal sank further into herself. She wished Ted would go away for a while and leave her with Bluebell. But Ted made it clear he would go nowhere.

The time her one remaining friend and her boyfriend came to visit, Ted made them feel so unwelcome that they soon left, never to return again.

When Petal insisted she was lonely, Ted reminded her that she had him. He would sulk and feign insult so Petal learnt to keep quiet and enjoy Ted's solitary company.

Sex had stopped as Petal could not face it, and poor Ted was heartbroken and rejected. Petal felt awful for destroying this beautiful, amazing man.

Petal would dress Bluebell but Ted would insist on changing her clothes. Petal learnt straight away that she must wait for Ted to choose baby Bluebell's clothes and then dress her.

Petal had collected some gorgeous bits for Bluebell, including baby lotions and potions, but Ted had thrown them away insisting she only bath and wash Bluebell in water with cotton wool.

Petal did as she was told.

Ted policed what Petal ate. When Bluebell was poorly, Ted would ask Petal what she had eaten, seeing as Bluebell only ever had breast milk.

Over the years poor Ted grew more and more unhappy. Petal begged him to tell her what she could do to help, but poor Ted explained that Petal had 'destroyed' him.

He explained that being with Petal had crushed poor Ted's confidence. You see, there had been absolutely nothing wrong with Ted before he met Petal. Petal had crushed him as a man.

Petal felt guilty so she bought some lovely underwear and asked Ted to try resuming their sex life, but poor Ted couldn't, he was crushed.

She begged him to come to counselling with her but he said he could fix it himself; he just needed to lift his confidence and not keep having all the constant drama and stress. Being with Petal had crushed poor Ted's confidence. You see, there had been absolutely nothing wrong with Ted before he met Petal. Petal had crushed him as a man.

Petal battled on. She had no friends and spent her weekends with Ted's mother, who she adored. Ted went away every weekend to work, but was always on the end of the phone instructing his mother and Petal on what to feed Bluebell and where they must take her and what they should do with her, and under no circumstances were they to feed Bluebell anything sugary!

Petal would never defy Ted. She had now realised that it was pointless. Ted never, ever, ever backed down, never in a million years, and Ted was always right.

Ted's mother would urge Petal to stand up to Ted but Petal knew it wasn't possible, because even his own mother did as she was told.

DAY FORTY-SEVEN

My knight in shining armour was a monster in disguise
The promises he made me turned into a pack of lies
He swore he'd never hurt me, like so many had before
Yet my knight in shining armour could not have hurt me more

Some days are harder than others in here. If you dislike one of the residents it's difficult. If you really like them then it's tougher. To like someone is to really care about them and to care is to really worry about them.

Sometimes I get pangs of guilt that I'm here with my beautiful, brave daughter beside me whilst others are here alone.

A couple of the lone women here at the refuge cling to one another and give each other the love and support they need when the staff go home for the weekend. I comfort myself with the belief that surely somebody had once loved these women, otherwise how would they know how to take care of each other?

Photographs emerge from handbags and coat pockets in this place. The proof of happier times. The women with their families and friends, laughing, stunning and vibrant, full of life. You can hardly recognise them now. Looking into their eyes you wonder when the pain and fear landed there. Is it there in the photo? Maybe, but then again, victims of domestic abuse are masters of disguise.

The physically abused will create a maze of lies and excuses to confuse and put off the concerned: 'Some people just bruise easily.'

Emotional abuse, while existing in the mind and not on the body, can be more difficult to conceal.

Some may avoid developing friendships just in case the friend becomes too close and sees behind the disguise. Friends may ask innocent questions that the abused is not comfortable answering.

The abuser will not allow these friendships to flourish and will often dissect the subjects discussed and the answers given.

I recall at this point how I would desperately try to create stories on my way back home from an outing with friends. I think back to my keep-fit classes: a little bit of exertion then over to the pub afterwards. Whenever I returned home my ex would bombard me with questions as to what we had talked about. If only he knew we had been discussing him!

My friends had often pointed out how controlling and undermining he was. Of course, I could never let him know any of that, so I would make up elaborate tales to tell him. Whatever the story I offered up, he would still get cross and suspicious saying, 'Keep-fit finishes at eight o'clock. It is now eleven-thirty which means you had approximately three hours in the pub. I'm sure you talked about other things. Perhaps there's a reason you're not telling me.'

This really used to spook me. Were there secret microphones planted on me?

Eventually I stopped going to keep-fit. And the pub.

. . . Things found a peaceful lull for a few months.

Petal's cherished grandmother sadly passed away, leaving a great big, posh house with a huge garden in the country. All of a sudden, Ted was happy to drive the one hundred miles to where Petal's parents lived to stay in her late-grandmother's house. Suddenly Ted couldn't do enough. He chopped down trees, he dug the garden, and he mowed the several acres of land.

He was kind and supportive to Petal's poor father who was heartbroken at losing his mother.

Ted's behaviour slightly baffled Petal, as Ted had not allowed Petal's parents to come and stay ever, and he had refused to let Petal take Bluebell to visit her parents or grandparents. By the time Petal's grandmother died, Bluebell was eight years old and had only met her great grandmother twice. But suddenly they spent every weekend at her grandmother's house. Ted happily spent each weekend in the company of Petal's parents and allowed them to take him out and buy him delicious meals.

One evening Petal and Ted were sitting at her grandmother's dining table and, for once, Ted seemed happy to listen as Petal poured out all the happy memories she had enjoyed with her grandparents at this very same table. The evening had been magical for Petal, particularly when a beautiful deer poked its face up close to the window.

Petal had wept for her grandmother that night and Ted had taken her into his arms and comforted her. Ted was her wonderful man again; he couldn't have been more loving.

Later that night he told Petal that if they could live in a house as perfect as her grandmother's then he would be all better and that they would all have a much better life. Petal couldn't believe what she was hearing. At last there was a solution and one that meant she could be with her beautiful Ted and Bluebell and her parents.

Oh, she hugged her knees close to her heart praying silently that her father would agree to let them rent the house from him. How stupid she felt; the solution, the answer to all their prayers had been staring her in the face and yet she hadn't realised. It all made sense.

Everything Ted had said all these years had been true. It was the house they lived in that made him miserable. It had been Petal who had made him miserable. But here, Petal made him happy. Here, Ted was confident and he was funny and handsome again and he felt so much better.

She had to make sure she got this for them.

Petal spoke to her father and he said he would see if there was any way they could arrange it so that Petal and Ted could live at the house but, alas, death duties were high and he had to sell grandmother's house.

As soon as the house was sold the visits to her parents ceased, hurting Petal and her parents all over again.

Ted returned to his previous state of mind and Petal went in search of her next quest in pleasing poor Ted . . .

Day Forty-Nine

Oh, we do like to be beside the seaside
We do like to be beside the sea
We do like to stroll along the Prom, Prom, Prom
Where we're nice and safe and the monster's gone

I had a lesson in life in a few short hours.

People who you may never come into contact with in normal life are suddenly all sandwiched together. Our mutual pain and fear uniting on a coach destined for the seaside.

The unbroken ones are full of life and are working hard to jolly us along. As the two refuge houses meet, we stare suspiciously at one another. Only the children seem oblivious to the atmosphere; today is all about having fun.

I choose to sit alone, painfully aware that my own daughter is not beside me. She's away on holiday with her father. I was determined to take this trip but somehow dread the reality.

I'm pleased that I can sit on my own on the coach, but I do position myself close to a woman and her son, who I have become very fond of. Her strength inspires me when I have none to keep going. This is her story . . .

HER STORY
HOW DID I GET HERE?

'How did I get here? How did I get here? . . .' Those five words reverberate desperately and pointlessly around my mind as I sit in this alien and empty room. I feel suffocated and trapped, paralysed by my perceived inadequacies and the bad choices I cannot re-make or undo. They haunt me daily; every time I shut my eyes I see a ghost from the past. I can barely breathe sometimes.

I can't pretend here. They know.

I sit in the room allotted to me, too scared to leave it. After a number of hours I sneak down to the kitchen but I'm caught; a lady is in the kitchen boiling the kettle. She smiles at me in a comforting, almost motherly way and I soon find that my fear of the other women abates. She asks no questions except to make sure that I have enough to eat and drink and she even offers me one of her milk tokens.

As time went on I learnt that this was an unspoken rule here: no-one spoke until they were ready to, and no-one pushed you to; yet you always felt people would listen should the time come.

The more time I spent alone, the more my mind became corrupted with dreams of the past and images of what might have been if I had just done this, or just said that. If I had been less weak or simply listened to those who had cared. I think I spend more time in that world than in the present one; the idea of happiness hasn't abandoned me here, though it is tempered by the insuppressibly bitter taste of futility.

They want me to talk, to bring me back. I'm scared that girl is gone, nothing's left.

The women here all have the same exhausted look; they are haunted by the same demons, the same fears and the same insecurities. Their grip upon each woman is different, though, and some almost seem to be beating them. I begin to realise that maybe I have a choice: I can continue to hope and wait for death, for release, or I can try. I need to try. Please let me try for my son.

I talk, they listen. There is no shock in their faces, no judgement in their tone. They've heard this before. I'm not alone in my pain, or in my self-doubt. There is no miracle cure, but there is help. I just have to be brave enough to take it.

I begin to talk to the other women here too; the refuge lounge often becomes something resembling group therapy as each woman entrusts her own experiences and losses with the others. Most women and children here escape with little or no possessions to their name. In this secret, close-knit environment the women and children become a community, helping one another through each day and each trial, even finding that ever evasive silver lining and sharing a laugh from time to time. I don't have to pretend here; they know.

I decided to see my GP; maybe she was wrong and taking medication for depression wasn't just something thick people did, as she had said to me with a smirk one day. 'Someone like you must find it hard in a place like that,' the GP said whilst reviewing my file. I was filled with rage. I felt defensive of the women I had met in refuge. There is no class system in there, no sense of superiority that inflates one's hopes or chances above another's, no particular social stratum from which inhabitants are either derived or mournfully relegated to. We were the same, we were people. How dare this woman assume that my pain must have been greater simply because I happened to have a BBC accent and a decent vocabulary? I had witnessed so much anguish in that house; a difficult background didn't somehow detract from your worth or inure you to suffering. She then expressed shock when she realised the man I was fleeing from was also a doctor. 'It really can be anyone,' she remarked unconvincingly, eyeing me up and down once again with renewed vacillation. I was stripped of my rage as self-doubt washed over me once again. I simply felt like a failure; she was a doctor, wasn't she? . . . Maybe it was my fault.

Unable to reason with myself, my confidence crushed, I begin to research. Even I can't argue with facts. It can be *anyone*. I immediately uncover horrific accounts of abuse committed by doctors, lawyers, teachers . . . and when I look at the women who have suffered at their hands, I simply feel their pain, I don't judge them. I don't investigate their position in the social hierarchy, look up their academic records or scrutinise their financial status to see if they deserve my sympathy. Of course I don't, so why am I judging myself? Just as this realisation dawns on me, so did another: there is a dangerous, pandemic ignorance on domestic abuse.

They set me up with some counselling. I continue my research . . .

I discover that, with my history of domestic violence, I represent one of a third of all womankind. With my self-doubt and tolerance of abusive behaviour I help make up the one in ten who thinks it is acceptable. I didn't realise I didn't deserve it, but I'm beginning to.

They saved me.

They say one in four gives up and tries to commit suicide; God grant those women peace and may they come to realise there is help before they make that choice.

I start again.

The road is hard and deep wounds leave great scars that stay with you and shape you. You will have good days and bad days, moments when the hill seems too steep and the light too far. But in those times you can call old friends; the team in refuge never leave you and check up on you when they can. They fight for you every day: in schools, with charities, with councils, in parliament and online.

Yet, in light of welfare cuts, changes in tax status and the near eradication of Legal Aid, they might just need you to fight for them one day, too.

When we arrive at the coast, our caring, unbroken angels carry bags laden with food and drinks to our picnic spot. Buckets and spades donated by 'a kind someone' are handed out to children who are fit to burst with excitement.

A couple of children hang back, unsure about enjoying such innocent fun. Perhaps their pain has been too much, they'll need more time to heal. Please, God, they will heal. We head to the beach, the rugs are laid down and the food is unpacked. Every choice of tasty morsel you can imagine!

The unbroken angels look on proudly at the scene before them. One little angel feels sand between her toes for the first time. She is so tiny but she screams with delight. I watch her mother's face in raptures by her daughter's new discovery and, for just a second, all the pain disappears from her face.

Each one of us gained something from this experience, I'm sure.

I sat drinking the warm tea and reflected on the times I had visited this very same seaside resort with my own daughter and her grandparents. I had no idea back then that I would return someday as part of a women's refuge. Don't get me wrong, I knew even then that I was unhappy and my ex-partner was utterly miserable with me, but was it really domestic abuse?

I remove the little card from my wallet and read it again to confirm the truth that I am indeed a victim of domestic abuse.

. . . Petal approached the council and looked into a house swap so they could still move to where her parents lived, seeing as Ted loved it so much there, but when she told him what she had done Ted announced there was no way he would move down there.

When Petal challenged him, he would have none of it. He had never said he would live down there.

When she argued that he had most definitely said that he would move there, he argued he had never agreed to move there.

When she reminded him that he had told his own mother they were contemplating moving there, he denied it and got angry.

Confused, bewildered and broken, Petal sank deeper into her shell.

Petal grew sadder and sadder. Her only solace was her dear little girl who was blossoming each and every day.

When Ted asked why Petal was crying so much these days, Petal said that she was sorry for making him so unhappy. She said that she couldn't cope with the feelings of guilt she was carrying around and how could she ever be able to make it up to him, knowing that she had crushed poor Ted.

Ted listened to her reasons for the tears and reinforced the message that she had indeed ruined his life. However, he was sure she could rectify it if she didn't cause anymore dramas for a while . . .

Day Fifty-Nine

Upside down, then back to front,
And, here we go again.
No chance of winning or escape
A sick computer game.

I am floundering.

I took a week away from the refuge with the aim being to spend some quality time with my daughter. What a joke that proved to be. Our attempt at a camping trip with friends was a disaster as I fell from one panic attack to another. There I was, dipping my head up and down like some kind of addict, gasping for air. I became so light-headed and faint that I kept laughing hysterically. The image of a glue-sniffer came to mind.

My wonderful friends helped protect my daughter from the embarrassment of seeing her mother desperately breathing in and out of a brown paper bag.

We cut the holiday short and returned to the refuge.

I fell apart and let my daughter stay with her father; anything to protect her from the mess I was in.

My support worker at the house called me in and I told her the truth. She asked me to go and meet with her and the refuge manager the following day.

. . . When Petal realised that all her attempts at fixing her and Ted were fruitless she decided to try to take back control of her life.

She had started psychotherapy with a new therapist who worked in the best clinic in London. Dr Miracle was amazing. Dr Miracle encouraged Petal to take back control of her life and to start doing her music and writing again. Petal missed writing songs so, so much, and so she got her keyboard out from under the bed. Ted was not happy and told her to put it back; that it took up too much space. Petal pointed out that Ted had slept on the sofa for the last ten years so the keyboard shouldn't get in his way.

Ted used the spare room for his music and said Petal could put the keyboard in there. She refused and kept it in her bedroom and started working on songs.

Two days later and poor Ted was at his wits' end. Petal's songs were depressing him. He asked why she couldn't write a happy song because her songs dragged his spirits down, which in turn prevented him from being able to work. He asked Petal not to sing her songs and play her music around Bluebell as he was worried it would have a negative effect on their daughter.

After not very long Ted had asked Petal to try to write when he and Bluebell weren't there but, alas, Ted was always there these days as he had lost a lot of work, which was Petal's fault. When she asked why she had caused him to lose so much work he explained . . . being with Petal had crushed poor Ted's confidence. You see, there had been absolutely nothing wrong with Ted before he met Petal. Petal had crushed him as a man.

Day Sixty

A pig and little pony
From Old Macdonald's farm
Locks and secret cameras
Keeping us from harm

I arrive at the 'other house' and I'm welcomed by the sights and sounds of a mini farm!

A local organisation has brought along a fine pig, a pony, some chickens and other assorted farmyard animals for the children to play with. The Shetland pony has had her mane plaited by one of the little angels who is beaming with delight. The dear little pony looks like something out of a children's comic.

This is something I find incredible about refuge life. The variety of healing support on offer in the shape of arts-and-crafts days, seaside trips and, indeed, animal farms, and the effort employed by everyone is endless and without exception.

Where would I be now if I had not met my own 'unbroken angel'? Not so long ago she gently – well, I say gently but I must admit she can hardly be described in those terms; I haven't met many like her. She has a wicked sense of humour and is brutally honest. Anyway, it was with her guidance that I made my way to this place of refuge. I smile as I recall her coming to court with me one time. I turned to her and said, 'I look a right mess, don't I?'

She laughed and said, 'You do look rough, but I've seen you look a lot worse!'

Not quite the answer I was hoping for, but the truth nonetheless.

I realise that I miss her as she works 'on the outside' and so I don't get to see that much of her. There were times 'on the outside', before I was ready for the refuge, when we would meet for coffee. Well, tea actually, but coffee sounds better somehow. I would be on my knees, fit to fall down or run away, but then I'd spend an hour in her company and my stomach would be cramped, not from fear but from laughter, and I would strut out of the café feeling recharged and ready to go again.

The meeting with the refuge manager takes place in her office with my key worker by my side. Cups of tea are shared round and they get me to breathe in and out of my paper bag again to calm myself down. These angels talk to me as though I am just like one of them, instead of a gibbering wreck, sucking the life out of this paper bag. I keep giggling as I get light-headed and they are kind enough to giggle with me.

As I drink my tea I recount my sorry tale. I tell them the truth, that I could not cope with the camping holiday and why. I tell them that I feel as though my arms are cut with deep slashes and my blood is pouring away.

Everyone keeps saying that it's just a little graze and that I am going to be fine. They tell me I am strong and brave.

The manager listens to me and replies cautiously: 'I cannot say you're going to be OK. We can only help you get through the next couple of weeks until your court case. I cannot promise you will win the court case because it's not down to me. I cannot stop you from running away and giving up; I can see you are completely wrung out. What I can tell you is that you will regret not seeing this process through. You have shown how brave and strong you are to get this far.'

. . . One miserable year followed another miserable year, and then another.

Eventually Petal decided to pluck up the courage and set Ted free. She assumed Ted would be relieved to be free from the awful life he was living with her but each time she confronted his unhappiness he would get angry, so she learnt to back down.

Ted was sick of her anxiety disorder which prevented her from travelling very far. He was sick of her insecurities and, above all else, he was sick to death of never having proper holidays as Petal was too agoraphobic to fly.

Ted's mother often spoke of her pity for poor Ted and poor Bluebell, that they couldn't get away on a proper holiday. When Petal tried explaining that she didn't mind them going without her, they both made her feel even guiltier. Couldn't she try, for Bluebell's sake? Surely, for Bluebell's sake, Petal could snap out of her anxieties and put her poor daughter first? And poor Ted hadn't had a proper holiday abroad in years and Petal knew how well it always made him feel to get away to the sun.

Petal was not only swamped in guilt for ruining poor Ted's life, but now she carried around the burden of ruining her poor daughter's life also. Petal lived in a permanent state of guilt and anxiety. Her panic attacks had become so intense that she thought they would kill her.

She knew Ted needed a holiday so was pathetically grateful when Ted's mother kindly treated them to a trip to Cornwall.

Ted had been furious and told Petal that he didn't want to go on holiday in this country.

When they arrived at the caravan park, Petal's heart sank to her shoes. The beautiful, glossy pictures they had seen in the brochure did not reflect the tired, shabby caravan park they drove through. Ted had already been miserable and angry. What would he be like now?

Ted was grinding his teeth and Petal knew he was getting angrier by the second.

Poor little Bluebell was clearly getting agitated and was desperately trying to jolly her daddy along. When that clearly wasn't working she joined in her father's scorn at the state of the place.

Petal put on her sing-song voice, desperately trying to shed a little light and humour into the situation.

The luxury caravan was all wrong.

The caravan park was definitely all wrong as they allowed dogs, and although Petal reassured him that their caravan was dog free and that all the dogs on site weren't allowed off leads, Ted could still smell them.

This holiday was quite an eye-opener for Petal, who was beginning to realise that Ted didn't like very much at all.

Ted didn't like dogs. He always said he did, but he didn't like them at all.

Ted didn't seem to like Cornwall very much.

Ted really didn't like England.

Ted didn't seem to like English women much either. Women from other countries were more confident and more sensual. Over the years Petal had managed to establish that Ted didn't seem to like the clothes she wore and he didn't like her hair much either. Petal tried and tried to change her appearance, her personality, her hair, her attitude, all of which were wrong. But stupid Petal couldn't get it right and just ended up making Ted even more miserable.

When Petal insisted that they could go on no longer and should part, Ted said it would need to wait as he had a bad neck and he couldn't possibly cope with any more worry at the moment.

'Surely, Petal, you've already caused enough damage; stress

has done this to my neck,' complained Ted.

'But Ted, I thought the doctor said it was a prolapsed disc,' replied Petal.

'It is, Petal, but because of all the stress you have put me through, my back and neck could not take any more.'

Oh poor, poor Ted, I've now damaged his spine, thought Petal.

When she tried to set him free a year later he said it needed to wait until he saved some money.

A further year passed and sadly Ted's father grew ill and died. Ted complained to Petal that he'd had to deal with his father's illness and death all by himself and had been left to grieve alone.

Petal was secretly furious with Ted as she had visited his father each and every day to cook for him, help keep his house clean and make sure that he took his medication. Ted's poor sister had given more than her share of time and effort to his father too, and yet Ted said he had done everything.

Ted was really not being fair, but Petal didn't argue as she had learnt so long ago never, ever to argue with Ted because Ted knew everything and was always right.

Two years later, after Petal felt she had given poor Ted long enough to grieve his loss, she tried to leave him again.

Petal realised that Ted didn't want to leave their council house but she explained to him that she was tied.

Ted had made it clear that he would never allow Petal to take Bluebell home to her parents.

Petal had no money and was not well enough to work. She was fortunate to receive disability benefits which helped support her financially, but it would never stretch to private rentals in the area.

When Petal pointed out that Ted had been left a considerable inheritance by his father and could easily afford to move out, he was furious. The argument escalated and Petal knew Ted would never physically hurt her but, even so, she didn't think it was wise to argue with him anymore today.

Petal ran without any shoes to her best friend's house.

Her friend calmed her down and Petal was comforted with the knowledge that Ted was going abroad that evening to work for a whole week, which would give her precious time with Bluebell.

During his week away Petal and Bluebell had a wonderful time, lazing around the house without being told off or controlled.

Petal chose to use this opportunity to appeal to Ted's mother for help. Petal loved Ted's mother so much. She said she would try to speak to Ted . . .

Poor Ted came home with a horrible virus and spent the next year in and out of hospital having tests. It seemed no-one could establish what was wrong with poor Ted. Eventually the doctors told Ted he had something very wrong with his liver. Petal felt terrible. Ted would need to be taken better care of now. She realised that the stress of leaving wouldn't help as Ted had said stress would aggravate it.

Petal still loved Ted and so she tried her best to nurse him through his long illness.

Another two years passed and Petal tried one more time to set Ted free, but poor Ted was at his wits' end. He said that they just needed to go and see a counsellor. So Petal spoke to Dr Miracle.

Dr Miracle had been gently but firmly building up Petal's strength and confidence. Each week Dr Miracle would challenge Petal's self-loathing and guilt, desperately trying to put together the fragmented pieces of her childhood and the parallels in which she was now living with Ted.

Dr Miracle said she would make a call and refer Petal and Ted *to the best couples' clinic in the country.*

When the appointment arrived, Ted was furious . . .

'But Ted, you said we needed counselling,' said Petal quietly.

'Yes, Petal, but not now. I meant in a couple of years when Bluebell has started secondary school; not now when I have a distinct lack of work coming in and I pay all the bills!'

Now Petal was cross. Ted did not pay all the bills. Petal bought all the food and more than made her contribution.

When Ted and Petal attended their first appointment at the posh clinic poor Ted explained to the counsellor that he was perfectly fine; it was Petal who had the problems. He explained to the counsellor that being with Petal had crushed poor Ted's confidence. You see, there had been absolutely nothing wrong with Ted before he met Petal. Petal had crushed him as a man.

The kind and patient counsellor listened to him; she asked him to tell her about his previous relationships and Ted took great pride in telling her what a wonderful partner he had been to his previous girlfriends. He announced that she could call any one of his ex-girlfriends who would give a glowing reference as to how he had been a good, decent boyfriend.

When she questioned Ted as to why he hadn't lived with anyone before Petal, he started getting twitchy and irritable.

The counsellor then turned her attention from him and asked for Petal's story; she asked about Petal's ex-partners.

Petal tried to keep it light and compare her ex-boyfriends to a bag of beanboozled jelly beans. When the counsellor looked confused, Petal explained that the sweets were a mix of delicious sweet flavours and disgusting flavours like vomit and cheese. She told her that she'd only managed to grab a couple of sweet ones before encountering the disgusting flavours.

The counsellor wanted more details and so Petal revealed how she had a few nasty boyfriends.

One had beaten her.

One had slept with a hammer at her head in case she left him.

Another one stole all her money.

Another one spiked her drinks to knock her out so that he could go and see his lover.

Petal giggled, embarrassed by the tale, and when the kind counsellor asked what she found so funny about it, Petal started crying. She was embarrassed and she couldn't quite believe what she was saying and felt the counsellor would judge her.

Petal explained how she couldn't live with the guilt any longer. She said that their relationship was over and that Ted refused to sleep in the bed with her and that Bluebell was beginning to make comments to people about the fact that Ted slept on the sofa. Petal told the counsellor that she felt sorry for Bluebell and that Ted had been furious with Bluebell for telling someone that Mummy and Daddy never slept together.

Petal hung her head in shame. She would never forget the way Bluebell had looked that day. She had been bewildered and embarrassed but had learnt from that moment on to keep quiet and never tell a soul. Petal explained how she and Dr Miracle were worried about the effect this would inevitably have on Bluebell.

Petal also said that she didn't believe Ted would ever do what was necessary to share a bed with her.

In front of the counsellor Petal put her hands together and begged Ted, for Bluebell's sake, to break up.

Ted had cried in front of the counsellor, great big tears, declaring his undying love for Petal and how he knew they could work things out. At the end of the session the counsellor explained to them both that she really couldn't help them, as for couples' therapy to work both parties had to come to the table with something. If it was all Petal's fault, then she couldn't help.

Ted seemed happy with the outcome. Poor Petal sunk further into despair.

They left the building and Petal would never forget the eye contact she had had with the counsellor before leaving; it was an eerie feeling. Was it perhaps a warning? No, Petal was being paranoid now.

As soon as they had left the posh clinic Ted was furious. During the walk back to the train station he told Petal just how angry he was that she had wasted all his time and money on fares getting into London and talking to a complete stranger about their relationship.

Petal apologised over and over again, reminding Ted that she had actually paid for the tickets, but Ted sulked and ignored her all the way back to their hometown station.

Once they got in the car he told her again how angry he was with her that she had wasted his time. Ted was furious and his chest puffed up like a huge peacock; his face went red and he punched the steering wheel and swore profusely.

Petal tried to sink into the car seat.

'Look at me, Petal. How much more are you going to put me through? You're going to kill me at this rate.'

Petal wept her heart out. Oh poor, poor Ted, what had she done to her beautiful man?

Dr Miracle, Petal's psychotherapist, had heard back from her colleague at the couples' counselling clinic and it seemed that she had just about had enough of the effect Ted was having on her patient. It had taken her a lot to get them a free consultation with the posh private clinic. Over the following months she started to be quite forceful with Petal about her relationship with Ted. This wasn't very useful for poor Petal at all as she was struggling to stay with him as it was.

Dr Miracle announced she would be retiring. Petal broke

down. She knew if she couldn't leave Ted with Dr Miracle beside her then she never would. She told Dr Miracle this.

Dr Miracle stared into Petal's eyes and asked, 'And one day, when your daughter brings home a man who treats her like her father treats you, how are you going to look her in the eye?'

If Dr Miracle had lain Petal down and then jumped full weight onto her stomach, she couldn't have winded Petal more.

Finally the day dawned. A line had been crossed and Petal knew there was no going back. It was time to end this pain and misery. The poison from their relationship had started seeping into the heart of her dear daughter.

Day Eighty-Nine (Part One)

Stripped of my dignity
Broken and bruised
Losing the strength I once had not to lose
Refusing to stoop to his level to win
I wait for my heart to be broken again

Living here is like travelling on a roller coaster in the dark. I have no idea where this ride will take me next. Will I be left upside down, back to front or inside out? I just know that it will all change again and I must hold on tight.

This morning my daughter is full of cold and I am brimming with anger. She should be at home, relaxing on the sofa watching TV and I should be pampering her and tempting her with tasty snacks. But instead we are here and he is still there.

It's one week until the final hearing and I am nervous.

Yesterday I received a phone call from my social worker revealing my ex-partner has stooped to yet a new low. He is now insisting I have supervised visits with my daughter every two weeks. He has more evidence to prove I am too mentally unstable to be a mother to my daughter. Apparently his mother has written a statement to back him up and has agreed that perhaps two hours on every second Saturday would be good for her granddaughter.

I'm scared because each and every day I dread what will

happen next. What will he do to me next? I'm tired now, I am so tired.

My best friend sent me a text yesterday begging me to 'Find one last bit of fight and anger from somewhere, please. This journey is not over.'

I'm holding onto her words right now, gripping hold so tight. I am feeling as vulnerable as a helium balloon in the hands of a tiny toddler. She could lose interest at any moment, seeing something else to take her fancy. Letting go of the ribbon, this balloon could be out of reach and left to drift for a million miles.

I ponder on these thoughts.

Maybe it would be simpler for all if I drifted out of their lives. I mean, my daughter and my family and friends would miss me, I've no doubt, but in some ways it might relieve the burden on all of them.

Even if I do get to go home with my daughter, how can I ever 'fix us'? How on earth am I going to salvage some sort of relationship with her when her father has convinced her that I am unstable and mentally ill?

People keep saying, 'You are strong and brave,' but I don't feel either of those things. The other broken angels are strong and brave, but me? No, I just don't get that right now.

Wallowing and self-pity surely cannot be good for the soul. I think I may combust soon! My support worker can see the full extent of my suffering today. She can see the hurt is no nasty little graze, but a deep, exposed wound that if neglected much longer may be too late to heal. She seeks out my daughter and talks to her in the kind, gentle manner that is her way. She finds me later and recounts the conversation. She tells me all is fine and that my daughter is looking forward to returning to school. She really is OK and she knows that I love her. This is what I need to hear.

I tell my daughter on a daily basis that I love her. I had

promised her years ago that I would resolve the misery, the endless arguments and the awful, oppressive atmosphere we suffered at home, and yet here we are, the best part of three years later and it's still going on.

. . . Ted and Bluebell had been playing on a games console in the lounge. They both started arguing as Ted accused Bluebell of cheating and poor Bluebell was trying to stand up for herself, promising that she hadn't cheated.

Petal's nerves were on edge these days. She walked into the lounge and said, 'For goodness' sake, you two, just switch the thing off if you're not enjoying it.'

Ted was furious. He threw the hand control down but it bounced off the sofa and straight into poor little Bluebell's face, causing her nose to bleed.

Ted was devastated by the accident and couldn't believe what had happened. Petal ran over and tried to comfort her daughter but Ted shoved her away. 'Don't you think you've already caused enough damage, Petal?' He then proceeded to explain to Bluebell that 'Mummy was responsible for this . . . Mummy needed to learn to shut up as it was because of what Mummy made him do that poor Bluebell's nose was bleeding.'

Petal sobbed that he could say such a horrible thing.

Poor little Bluebell was devastated.

Petal kept arguing over and over that it wasn't her fault; how on earth could he blame her for that? Ted said what he constantly said these days: 'Oh Bluebell, Mummy knows exactly what she is doing.'

Petal couldn't cope any longer. She needed help. She reached out to Ted's mother and his sister. She told them everything and they both agreed that Ted should seek some kind of anger management. His mother announced that Ted had always been angry and that she would try to speak to him, but didn't. She couldn't because she never stood up to Ted and always did what she was told.

Petal knew she needed to get Bluebell away from the toxic cloud they were all living under and spent the whole week begging Ted to let her go, pleading with him to help end their relationship amicably for the sake of their beautiful Bluebell.

Bluebell had asked Petal why Daddy was so angry and what was wrong with him. Petal promised Bluebell that she would sort things out and that she would make it all stop.

Petal told Ted what Bluebell had said but he didn't believe her.

Petal said she wanted it to be over. Ted was having none of it. He got up from the sofa and got angry. He threw things and smashed things and when the anger didn't make Petal retreat, he dropped to his knees and begged and cried great big tears, spilling down his face and bubbling from his nose.

Through the tears Ted could see that Petal was not going to back down. He stood up and the tears miraculously disappeared.

Then it happened. Something that was so disturbing that it reminded Petal of the eye contact she had had with the counsellor . . . Suddenly Petal realised what the sensation was, the day Dr Miracle had asked her how she would look Bluebell in the eye. The look the counsellor had given her and now this moment, it was the terrifying twist in the movie. The film you spent the duration believing you knew what was going to happen and then, BANG, just like that, it's completely different to what you thought and it's so, so creepy.

Ted calmly spoke to her and asked if she was serious. When she replied yes, he said: 'I will ask you one more time, are you serious?'

Petal looked Ted straight in the eye and replied, 'YES.'

Ted started to laugh in a disturbed, almost deranged manner.

*He began rubbing his hands together as he came close to Petal's face, and in a strange, creepy voice said, 'Oh now, Petal, this is when things start to get **really** interesting, really interesting indeed. You have no idea.'*

DAY EIGHTY-NINE (PART TWO)

> Daddy keeps on playing
> Daddy's having fun
> Mummy keeps on crying
> 'Cause he won't stop till he's won

My daughter announces that she feels better and wants to see her father. I drop her off at a local shopping centre where they've arranged to meet. As we drive off I realise that I have just spent the last twenty-four hours with a virtual stranger.

We pull up at the shopping centre and I watch that virtual stranger run straight into her father's arms and laugh. She looks into his eyes and chatters away to him. I observe a happy, relaxed twelve-year-old enjoying the company of her father; very different to the uncomfortable, nervous child who stayed with me last night.

I had spoken to my support worker about how guarded my daughter seems to be around me and she reminds me of all the awful things he has told her.

I think of the last year we all spent together in that house. He would tell my daughter that I wasn't safe. He told her how I left doors open at night and how I left the gas on and candles burning. My poor daughter must have been so terrified of having an imposter turn up in the middle of the night or of being burnt alive in her own bed.

He told my daughter that I stole from him and placed ridiculous amounts of locks and bolts on the spare bedroom door, where he kept his belongings. My daughter grew suspicious of me. She was allowed to know where the key was but not to 'tell Mummy'.

I go to a café to have something to eat and the tears keep rolling like waves. People are staring and I am not sure what concerns me most: the fact that the tears refuse to stop or that I couldn't care less who sees them.

I remembered when my cousin came to visit: 'What's happened to you, gorgeous? Where'd you go to? For goodness' sake, gorgeous, grab life by the throat and live it to the max!'

I shudder, because if he could see me now he most definitely would not recognise me. I am so lost that I may as well be living in some parallel universe, like I did as a child.

. . . Petal knew there was no going back. She had told Ted the truth: that she was leaving him. He wasn't the only miserable one. Petal and her poor daughter Bluebell were in the depths of despair and enough was finally enough.

Unfortunately for Petal, as her determination to leave Ted grew, so did his determination to put Petal firmly back in her place.

Ted had money but Petal didn't. The money Ted did have was his inheritance from his father and there was no way that Petal would take a penny of it.

Ted upped the stakes in his bullying campaign, which now included denying Petal the right to use hot water or any electricity. He would march into her bedroom and demand she turn off the lights. Ted knew Petal was terrified of the dark.

Sometimes if Petal was asleep, Ted would come in and lift the duvet off her and stare at her. She would wake, terrified, but pretend to be asleep. This really had a dramatic effect on Petal's anxiety, triggering old memories.

He would follow her from room to room, picking on her, shouting at her and demanding money from her.

Meal times had grown increasingly difficult. Petal made a delicious chicken casserole but it was during August . . .

'What is this, Petal?' he asked.

'It's chicken casserole, Ted.'

'I wasn't asking what the food was, I was asking what is it?'

Petal looked nervously to Bluebell, who was wearing an expression that Petal was seeing far too frequently these days: that of a child wanting to go and hide behind the walls, just as Petal had at Bluebell's age.

Ted took a mouthful of casserole and spat it out.

'It's summer, Petal, it's boiling. I can't eat this. This is winter food, not summer food. What the hell are you cooking this for?'

'I'm sorry, Ted.' Secretly Petal had wanted to tell Ted to stick the casserole where the sun don't shine, but poor Bluebell looked terrified, as though she needed to say something too.

'Mummy, why have you cooked this meal on such a hot day?'

Oh, and how Ted reached across and kissed his little loyal disciple, so proud was he of her comments. He was teaching her well.

Petal never took what poor little Bluebell said to heart, for she knew that Bluebell had become so nervous of an outbreak at any moment and was desperate to calm the storms that raged within Ted.

The next day, Petal decided to make Ted the salad of all salads. There was rocket, spring onions and crisp iceberg, watercress, cucumber and shiny cherry tomatoes, all topped off with salmon and tiger prawns. As she proudly placed the meal before Ted, Bluebell stared nervously at her father.

'What is this, Petal?'

'It's salad, Ted; it-it-it's summer food like you asked for.'

'Stop stammering and pretending you're scared of me, Petal.'

'I'm n-n-not, T-Ted.'

'Look at my hands, Petal; I'm shaking. For, goodness' sake, Petal, I need meat. I can't keep going on this; look at me shaking.'

The following day Petal tried a dish with ham and chicken.

'No, no, no, Petal. What is this?'

'It's meat, Ted.'

'Petal, I wouldn't call ham meat. There is as much meat in ham as there is in a loaf of bread; it's all reformed rubbish.'

'But Daddy, there's chicken breast, too,' poor little Bluebell said bravely.

Ted glared at Bluebell. 'Bluebell, chicken is not meat; it is pumped full of hormones.'

Ted looked triumphant and Petal knew that one of his lectures was coming on and would last the duration of the evening.

Poor, poor Bluebell.

The next day Petal prepared burgers but they were wrong; so the following day she bought rump steak but poor Ted said it nearly pulled his teeth out when he tried to chew it; so the next day she bought tender fillet steak.

'Now this, Petal, is what I call meat.' Oh and how Ted rejoiced, at last silly Petal had got something right.

Petal served Ted the same meal every day for the next month and he was most satisfied.

One day, not long into September, Ted patted his tummy and asked Petal what she was feeding him. 'I'm piling on the weight here, Petal!'

'Well if you don't mind me saying, Ted, you do eat an awful lot of biscuits.'

'I do nothing of the sort, Petal, I hardly have any.'

Petal tried to stand her ground. 'Well, Ted, I d-d-do buy a packet of biscuits every two days and I only eat a couple a day. You don't let Bluebell eat biscuits during the week and she only has one at the weekend.'

'Well I don't eat them,' Ted replied. Conversation over.

A week later the mystery of the phantom biscuit eater was solved. Ted found Petal in the kitchen and he looked like thunder.

'Petal, would you please stop buying all this rubbish and leaving it for me to see in the cupboards.'

'But Ted, you don't need to eat it just because it's there,' she said bravely.

'Ah but I do, Petal, and d'you know what? Anyone would think that you're deliberately trying to fatten me up.'

'Why on earth would you think that, Ted?' Petal was shaking and desperate to hide it from him as it really annoyed Ted when she stammered and shook.

The atmosphere at home had become so intolerable. She knew she needed to do something.

Petal had a long-cherished friend called Frank who knew exactly what poor Petal and Bluebell were going through. Frank's own mother had been a victim of domestic abuse and he knew only too well what this was doing to mother and daughter. Frank often let Petal stay in his beautiful home; she loved it there as she felt safe and cared for. It had fairy lights that twinkled at night saying all was well.

Poor Petal wished to care for Bluebell but Ted would not let her. Ted stopped Petal from reading to her daughter, allowing her only thirty seconds to say goodnight to the child before insisting that Petal remove herself from the bedroom so that Bluebell could sleep. Ted would then stand beside the bed talking to Bluebell for another half an hour, leaving Petal to sit and listen as he bullied and manipulated the child.

Ted knew all about the incident that Petal endured as a child. When they had first met she told him about all the intimate details from her psychotherapy sessions. Ted had made notes. It was becoming clear to Petal that Ted's full intention was to use her childhood experience to hurt her and frighten her daughter.

The last Christmas they spent together as a family had been the most disturbing. Ted had become so angry and obsessive; he ranted and he raved around the house, throwing things and telling their beautiful daughter that it was 'all Mummy's fault' and that, as usual, 'Mummy ruined everything.'

Early Christmas morning, Ted refused to sit with his daughter whilst she opened her stocking. Petal pleaded with him quietly to just try, for Bluebell's sake, to be pleasant. But no, Ted was hell bent on making it the most miserable Christmas any of them had ever had.

Later that day they arrived at Ted's mother's house and, once again, the ugly face disappeared and the handsome, charming mask took over. Petal found this transformation quite disturbing and was reminded of a song she had written about Ted some time ago. The song was called 'Two Faced' and the first line began: 'You look good enough to eat, but I have seen the ugliness you wear on your other face'. Petal repeated this mantra, singing it over and over again in her head simply to get her through this miserable Christmas.

Petal spoke to her wonderful, patient doctor in the New Year. She advised her to seek help through the Domestic Abuse Helpline. Petal was astonished. 'But Ted has never hit me, I'm not a victim of domestic abuse; we're just not compatible that's all.'

Her doctor smiled kindly and said to check it out anyway.

Petal found the website and answered a few questions. She was amazed as there, staring back at her from the screen, was proof that she was indeed a victim of domestic abuse. In the end it was all the confirmation she really needed.

A great strength surged through Petal's body and she dialled a number.

A woman named Gabriel returned Petal's call and they arranged to meet. When they talked together Petal knew that Gabriel was her guardian angel. It may take a few more months to finally leave Ted, but Gabriel was waiting to fly her to safety.

The local council had granted Petal council accommodation years before when she hadn't been able to work due to her anxiety disorder which, at times, left her unable to leave the house. Petal had been persuaded to put Ted's name on the tenancy and both Ted and his mother had assured Petal that under no circumstances would Ted take away his daughter's and her mother's home.

Ted was now attempting to take the house and steal away her daughter too. Unfortunately, like all of Ted's other promises, this one had not been kept.

They tried mediation, but it failed miserably as Ted would not agree to anything. During the last appointment Ted had sat and cried and cried, declaring his undying love. Petal had been mortified and told Gabriel when she met her.

'Oh Petal, that's not love. You wouldn't treat a dog the way that Ted treats you.'

'But Gabriel, he's just so heartbroken.'

'Of course he is, because he is losing his control. Ted's a bully. He has bullied you for years, Petal. Do not confuse control and power with love.'

Petal realised that the only option left to her was to move Bluebell away from her school and her friends, and move back home. Home was over a hundred miles away but at least she would have family there.

When she told Ted, he made it perfectly clear that he would call the police and cause as much damage as he could. Petal knew Ted would keep that particular promise and so she decided to try to stay put.

Sadly things reached a peak and Petal knew she could take no more. Her solicitor told her she should go to court to ask them for an 'occupation order' which would mean that Ted would have to vacate the house.

Gabriel and Meg, Petal's beautiful, loyal friend, went to court with her and supported her. They patiently sat with her, making her laugh and building Petal's strength in order to get through the ordeal.

The judge decided that an occupation order was 'most draconian' and he was unwilling to make an order to remove Ted from his own home. However, he was willing to grant a non-molestation order which would not allow Ted to enter Petal's bedroom, and would prevent him from pestering or harassing her.

Petal broke down in Gabriel's arms where she was gently comforted.

The barrister explained how the non-molestation order would protect Petal at home but both Gabriel and Petal knew that Ted would never, ever change his behaviour. The non-molestation order would just ignite Ted's fury; and ignite Ted's fury it did, with big shiny bells on.

Her solicitor made it clear that Petal was not to leave the house but Ted would taunt Petal; the pestering and harassing grew to new heights.

Ted was fond of burping in Petal's face. Or he would walk into the room where she was, break wind and then leave.

He constantly sucked his teeth near Petal's face to the point that she suggested he tried flossing to prevent the irritating sucking noises.

Answering back would provoke his temper and things would be thrown and broken.

He started to drag their poor daughter Bluebell into these pointless confrontations and he threatened to tell Bluebell all about the 'disgusting thing' that had happened to Petal when she was a girl. Petal was desperate; she knew that no child would want to hear about her mother's terrible childhood experience. She knew she must protect her.

During one particularly unpleasant row, Petal's best friend telephoned her. Petal discreetly answered her phone, leaving it on so that her friend was able to hear the entire conversation.

When Ted saw Petal put the phone to her ear he panicked. All the colour drained from his face. The swearing and shouting stopped immediately. Ted was getting really good at controlling his temper when others were around or within earshot. Except for poor little Bluebell; sadly, she was subjected to both barrels.

Petal's friend asked where Bluebell was.

'Here,' answered Petal.

'Did Bluebell listen to any of that?'

'Every word,' replied Petal.

DAY ONE HUNDRED & TWO

The path to freedom is yours to choose
The cost? Your children, prepare to lose
He'll tell them you're crazy, he'll make you look bad
He'll tell, when they listen, that Mummy's gone mad

The Freedom Programme is a domestic violence programme created by Pat Craven. It evolved from her work with perpetrators of domestic violence. It provides information, not therapy.

The Programme was primarily designed for women as victims of domestic violence, since research shows that the vast majority of cases of serious abuse are male on female. However, the Programme, when provided as an intensive two-day course, is also suitable for men, whether abusive and wishing to change their attitudes and behaviour, or victims of domestic abuse themselves.

The Freedom Programme examines the roles played by attitudes and beliefs on the actions of abusive men and the responses of victims and survivors. The aim is to help them to make sense of and understand what has happened to them, instead of the whole experience just feeling like a horrible mess. The Freedom Programme also describes in detail how children are affected by being exposed to abuse and, very importantly, how their lives are improved when the abuse is removed.

I've just attended my second week of the Freedom Programme.

As I sat and absorbed each and every story I reflected on my own sad tale. At once I understood that while they are completely different, they are also entirely the same.

. . . Her best friend arrived at the house as Ted came rushing downstairs ranting.

Her friend calmly announced that she would indeed speak to Ted, but outside, where Bluebell could not hear them. The conversation lasted an hour in the bitter cold and her poor long-suffering friend was exhausted when she finally rejoined Petal.

She told her that Ted had some pretty warped views and that he seriously felt that Petal was not a fit parent. Her best friend, strong and pretty insouciant, looked worried today, really worried.

Petal told her beautiful GP how her solicitor had told her not to vacate the house as it was playing into Ted's hands; how Ted was using the fact that Petal was too frightened to sleep at the house when he was there as a tool to prove what an unfit mother she is. Her GP said she felt the same as Dr Miracle; they needed to keep Petal well and safe. Petal's struggle with her anxiety disorder was already beginning to buckle under the pressure of it all.

During this difficult time Gabriel spent each week listening to and reassuring Petal that all would be OK. She told her that the refuge would be a good place for her and her daughter to move to, but Petal was still unsure. She was scared of the very prospect of a refuge; what if it was a horrible, scary place? Gabriel tried to reassure Petal that a refuge is a place of safety and that the staff work hard to ensure all residents feel secure. Gabriel explained how security cameras are in operation at all times and the residents even have to sign an agreement never to disclose the address of the place.

Petal said she would go if Gabriel would come too.

Gabriel laughed; she couldn't. She could only promise to visit as her job was to support the broken angels on the outside. Petal decided that if Gabriel was going to be selfish and wasn't going then neither was she! Poo sux Gabriel.

Gabriel laughed out loud with a beautiful twinkle in her eye which was her mischievous spark.

Petal had another reason not to go. People had already voiced their shock, including Ted and his mother: what sort of a mother would people think she was for taking her child to a refuge?

One day Petal knew she could take no more. Ted's behaviour had almost become deranged by now. With Petal's permission, Gabriel had spoken to Petal's solicitor and explained just how bad things had become. Petal's beautiful GP also wrote to her solicitor expressing her concerns about the effect this was having on Petal and Bluebell.

Petal's solicitor reminded Petal that the courts had granted a non-molestation order to protect her. Ted was not allowed in her bedroom and he wasn't allowed to bully and pester her. She made it clear that unless Petal enforced the order then there was nothing she could do. The court hearing could be weeks, even months away.

Petal cried, 'But Gabriel, he's enjoying himself, it has all become a game. He comes in and shouts at me and taunts me and then tells me to tell my solicitor. He thinks there is nothing they can do to him.'

'Then, Petal, maybe it's time you got the order enforced. You need to call the police,' replied Gabriel.

Petal was horror struck. 'Oh Gabriel, I couldn't. I mean he's not hitting me or anything; he's just being Ted.'

'If you don't enforce this order then I'm afraid Ted will continue to enjoy himself at your expense.'

Petal knew this was wise advice and, when eventually Ted's behaviour became intolerable, she decided to enforce the non-molestation order.

DAY ONE HUNDRED & EIGHTEEN

I'm leaving, I'm crying, I'm floating, I'm trying
To leave my safe haven and stumble on home
I'm feeling so tiny, so scared, so alone

I packed our things and moved everything out. I should have been ecstatic but all I felt was intense pain.

One of the refuge managers was there. I didn't want her to be; she was too important, too special. Her soul runs deep through each member of staff and every mother and child who enters here.

I've watched others come and go. You are given boundaries when you reside here. Some have broken the rules and have had to leave, not as a punishment but to ensure the safety of all who seek refuge here.

I look at the manager now and think about how she and the other manager make every possible attempt to help us, the broken angels. During our time here they are determined we know how it feels to be safe, to feel important and worthwhile. I know that it takes away a little piece of them if they lose even one of us.

I want to hug her, so I do, but it doesn't make me feel any better. It just makes the pain more intense. I think she is genuinely over the moon that I am finally going home where we can start to rebuild the life both my daughter and I deserve. I stumble over my thanks but it feels so lame.

For the first time ever I had felt safe, respected and understood. How could I just walk away from this sacred place and leave it all behind? I couldn't find the words to express my gratitude or to describe what I was feeling so I burst into tears instead.

. . . Petal told her best friend what she would need to do. Poor Petal was grief stricken. In spite of how awful Ted was treating her, there was still a part of her that loved him. How could she not love the man who had given her beautiful little Bluebell?

She sat in a café, desperately struggling with her conscience. How could she ask them to arrest poor Ted?

What if she stayed until Bluebell was sixteen?

As soon as she asked herself the question, she knew that it wasn't an option. She knew that the longer this continued, the weaker she would become. The weaker she became, the less use she would be for her daughter. The less use she was for her daughter, the more she would struggle with her guilt. The more she struggled with her guilt, the more poorly she became. The more poorly she became, the more ammunition she gave to Ted.

She took a huge breath, paid her bill and walked up the hill to the police station, each step feeling as though she were walking in quicksand, dragging her under.

At the police station she was asked to go into an interview room. Petal struggled to get the words out between trying to breathe and trying not to cry, but eventually she managed to reveal why her solicitor had told her to enforce the order.

There were two police officers present. The younger police officer made Petal feel so silly.

'So he doesn't let you have any electric on?' the young officer enquired.

'That's right,' Petal answered, trying to remain calm.

'Can you give an example?' the other officer asked.

'Well he'll come into my bedroom when I'm there and switch off the light and the radiator, and he knows he isn't allowed in my room; I have a non-molestation order forbidding him to come into my bedroom.'

'So why don't you ask him to leave and put the light and radiators back on?' the older officer asked.

'I can't, because Ted gets angry.'

'Does he hit you?'

'No.'

'Does he hit your daughter?'

'No.'

'So why are you afraid of him? What does he do?'

'He sulks.'

At that the young officer looked at the older officer and burst out laughing at the thought of arresting a man because he doesn't allow the electricity on and he sulks!

He stopped long enough to ask Petal why she didn't just ignore him. Petal tried to make the officer understand that she tries and tries but Ted was beginning to take it out on Bluebell instead.

The older police officer then asked why she didn't get herself and Bluebell out of the house when he acts like this. Petal explained that Ted wouldn't allow her to take Bluebell away and that in order to protect her daughter she would stay at home until her daughter was in bed, then she would drive to her friend's house and stay there the night and drive home in the morning. She explained that Ted was using her absence at night against her as evidence of her being an unfit mother as she was never at home.

The young officer asked another question: 'So why not just stay in your room and ignore him?'

Exasperated Petal said, 'I try to but he comes in and . . .'

Petal couldn't finish her sentence. She was aware of the officer giggling again and she supposed it did all sound rather comical. But when you put the events into perspective, when you multiply the events . . .

Five times a day.

Seven days a week.

Three hundred and sixty-five days a year . . . it's not so funny now, is it?

She thought back to what Gabriel had told her: 'Until you live with a domestic abuser you can be unaware of the damage they can cause a person. The slightest behaviour whether it be a glare or a gesture is enough to put their victims firmly back in their place.'

Petal left the police station feeling utterly deflated. She called her solicitor and Gabriel who both said how badly the police officer behaved. Petal said she couldn't really blame him as it did sound funny in some ways.

Petal visited her best friend who, as usual, popped on the kettle and stopped whatever she was doing to support her friend. With her batteries recharged, Petal was determined not to give up so she returned to the police station the following day.

This time she met a different officer who was very sympathetic and made it a lot easier for her. He understood immediately that Ted had broken the non-molestation order and assured Petal that Ted would be arrested the following morning. The police officer promised he would do everything in his power to make sure that Bluebell was safely out of the way at school. He advised Petal to take Bluebell to stay at her friend's as it was possible that Ted would be released fairly soon after.

Just as the officer had said, Ted was arrested the following day. Petal had collected a bewildered Bluebell from school and explained that they needed to stay with their friends until a space in refuge became available.

Poor Bluebell was mortified, confused, resentful. Her anger towards her mother was clear. Petal knew that Bluebell had every right to be angry. Petal also knew that Ted would make sure that he appeared the victim. Still Petal refused to be horrible about Ted in front of Bluebell. She did, however, make it clear that Ted could not continue to treat Petal the way he did, particularly in front of Bluebell.

Petal and Bluebell were safely at her best friend's house when Ted was released a few hours later; there was no evidence to hold him and it was Petal's word against his.

Gabriel assured Petal that the refuge was looking for a place for her and her daughter and that they should have somewhere to go within the next two weeks.

Ted kept turning up at the friend's house, crying. This made poor Bluebell so uncomfortable with the situation and Petal was devastated. She just couldn't believe she'd involved the police and had him arrested when she saw poor Ted standing outside looking so sad.

Petal's friend reassured her that there really was nothing else she could have done, seeing as Ted was hellbent on pushing the boundaries beyond healthy for all of them.

Eventually the day dawned when Gabriel let Petal know the good news: her colleague Sparkle would be calling to offer Bluebell and Petal a room at the refuge. Petal arranged to meet Gabriel in their special café where they chatted about all of Petal's fears.

Petal and Bluebell finally moved into the refuge. It was strange at first and poor Bluebell was most uncomfortable to begin with. The caring staff there knew exactly what they were doing and it really didn't take too long before Petal's daughter couldn't wait to return there each day.

Gabriel called in soon after to see Petal, who said she couldn't believe she hadn't been persuaded to go earlier.

'It had to be your choice, Petal! All I could do was guide you and let you know that there really were options. There is a safe place for women and children to reside, but you have to take those first steps; I cannot make those decisions for you.'

Petal did love Gabriel. She was funny and blunt and strong. She knew Gabriel needed to go and take care of the other broken angels on the outside but she still promised to keep in touch. Petal learnt that, just like Florence and Joan, the refuge managers, Gabriel tried her best never to break her promises.

During their stay at the refuge, Petal and Bluebell made some wonderful, interesting friends. Petal had hoped to cope with their situation but she had never expected to actually enjoy herself living amongst the broken angels.

With somewhere safe to live and with all the support on hand, Petal felt more able to cope with Ted's continual onslaught. It was becoming obvious that he would not rest until he had completely rubbished poor Petal's character and good name.

The social worker who had been assigned to meet with Ted and Petal to decide the fate of dear little Bluebell had announced that she thought Ted was a far better parent and that dear little Bluebell would be better off living with him.

Ted and his family bombarded the social worker with letters to dismiss Petal as a drunken, unfit mother. Ted also used Petal's old psychotherapy notes he had taken to show the social worker just how unwell Petal had been. The social worker had looked down her nose at Petal, informing her that she didn't look good on paper at all.

Fortunately Petal's beautiful doctor had been way ahead

of Ted. The previous year she had arranged for Petal to have a psychiatric assessment which clearly stated that Petal was a most fit parent and not mentally ill at all.

Petal believed that wonderful people, guardian angels in fact, had been watching over her, gently and discreetly guiding her towards Gabriel who had been determined to fly her to safety. She never once gave up on Petal and Bluebell, even when it didn't feel as though there was a great deal left of Petal.

Ted upped his smear campaign against Petal. She kept her dignity and refused to stoop to his level. When Ted ran out of ways to destroy Petal, he decided to start on the company she kept and tried to discredit her friends and, in particular, her friend Frank . . .

FRANK'S STORY

Most of my earliest memories are vague, however they are painfully real.

I do know that my mother, my siblings and I fled an abusive man. He was the father to my two younger brothers. The details aren't clear to me but I know it happened.

We fled to another place but, soon after, another man entered our lives.

When I look back to my childhood, I can't recall a time when he wasn't there. I believe that I was four when Gordon came to live with my mother and us children in our two-bedroom council flat in Battersea. There were four children and two adults crammed in this small flat.

This man came across as a reasonable person at first

but it was not long before he started abusing my mother and, by default, us children. He would beat her and tell her how worthless she was and steal her money.

I was the only one who ever stayed in the room when the beatings would occur, usually on the slightest pretence. She may have 'spoken out of turn' or he couldn't find something of his. I would shout and scream but I couldn't stop it; I was too small.

He only beat me once. Great, deep wounds inflicted by a curtain wire. He was cutting my hair at the time. He convinced my mum that she should pay him to do it rather than pay the barber. My mother had not been home when it happened. She had been in hospital for a routine operation. I remember playing outside on the streets afterwards, the whip lashes clearly on show for everyone to see, yet they all pretended not to.

That's what it was like back then, where we lived. People turned a blind eye, anything to avoid being dragged into a domestic quarrel. Strangely, he had the confidence to let me out to play with the wounds clearly visible. Either he knew no one would care or he was twisted enough to believe that he hadn't done anything wrong. What bothers me more these days is that after the pain had stopped, it wasn't such a big deal to me. I was able to get on with being a child playing with broken cast-off toys in the flats where we lived with my wounds on show. He didn't even get me to put on a top to hide what he had done.

I had learnt from an early age that even if the police were called there was not a damn thing they would do about it. There was always an excuse not to take action over domestic abuse. But, then again, my mother would never press charges; she just wanted him to stop hurting her. The one time she did get him removed, he soon came back, despite an injunction. Back into our home to carry on oppressing our family.

I remember the day I came home from school and saw him sat on our sofa; my heart sank. I told him that I would call the police as I assumed that he'd come back of his own accord. But he hadn't. She had allowed him back. When he told her what I said about calling the police, my mother got angry with me and told me off. I learnt that even if I did try to protect my mother it would be of no use because it seemed that she was prepared to defend him over us. I was heartbroken; I couldn't believe that she let him back after getting him removed. I felt betrayed. Why didn't my mother take the opportunity to move on and forge a better life for us all? I didn't understand until later in life why she felt that she didn't deserve better and why someone would make those choices.

My mother and Gordon slept on a sofa bed in our lounge. One of the bedrooms, which I shared with my sister until I was about eight or nine, was off the lounge. We had to walk through the lounge to get to our bedroom. I didn't usually dare get out of bed to go to the toilet after they had turned the light out. My sister developed a bed-wetting problem as she was too scared to walk through the lounge.

By the time I was six or seven all my mother's teeth were false. The beatings were so severe he'd knocked them all out. I don't ever remember him trying to be apologetic, loving or remorseful. My memories of him are that of an evil, sadistic bully. He was a child in a man's body. In my experience, abusers often have a childish mentality.

Perhaps that's why they can kid themselves that what they are doing isn't their fault. Usually children will come up with all sorts of excuses so they can't be blamed for their actions.

My brothers and I couldn't stop him beating my mother; we were too small. We watched, powerless that we could do nothing. We were all trapped within the miserable walls and soon my brothers and I decided to stay out of the way. The other option was unbearable.

We would often stay out late roaming the streets. The only other kids that stayed out with us were the kids that didn't want to go home either, for their own reasons. Some, just like us, escaping the oppression, and some just plain neglected. In fact we were all neglected. No-one came looking for us if we were out late. No-one cared enough. I can't imagine what I would feel today if I saw a bunch of seven- to ten-year-olds wandering the streets in London late at night unaccompanied. But that's what it was like back then. Even the police on patrol wouldn't take any notice of us unless we were doing something wrong.

Kids like us didn't usually perform well at school. We were blamed for any trouble even if it hadn't been us. When you are treated like you are nothing but trouble, you eventually perform to the standard others have set for you. Of course we were disruptive, but what did we know? We didn't come from orderly loving environments. We were very poor and neglected. The stigma of being from a one-parent family – four mixed-raced kids with three dads between them – the odds were against us from the start. Added to the fact that, in the end, we didn't have any option but to return home not knowing what we'd be walking in to.

There were times when Gordon wouldn't be home. Sometimes he could be gone for a few days. Those times would be the best we could hope for. We could watch what we wanted on TV. My mum would be more relaxed and being home was OK. The problem was that we didn't know when he would return.

Back then there were no women's refuges. There wasn't much help, if any, for people like my mother. We had nowhere to escape to. She was at his mercy. The poor woman had no respite; no-one to step in. Her own mother and father as well as one of her sisters rejected her because of the shame of her status of being an unmarried mother with 'half-caste' children. That was the term for mixed-raced children back then.

As we became 'problem children' (especially me), social workers were called in, but they were only concerned with the trouble we had caused and certainly not the reasons why we had caused the trouble. In hindsight, had they focused on the reasons behind the behaviour, then perhaps a few others could have been saved. I recently discovered that a lot of the people I hung out with way back then have either died, turned to drugs or are in prison serving long or life sentences. Only a couple managed to turn their lives around like I did.

My father occasionally appeared, like a movie star to a child, in his posh Mercedes but not giving me or my mother anything to help raise his child. I can remember at that time being impressed by him and yet now I look back at him with utter contempt. Contempt for his continual absence from my life. He was a tall, strong man; he could have stopped the bully who reigned over my mother and her children and yet he chose to selfishly turn a blind eye, easing his conscience, perhaps, with the occasional crumb of affection towards me. The only thing he bought me, as I remember it, was a Chopper bike. Not many children had these bikes. This reinforced my belief that he was a good father. He had bought me an extravagant gift which meant to me that he cared. At the time those bikes cost over £30. That was nearly forty years ago.

But that was it. Period. I cannot recall a thing else that he did for me.

I recall my brothers and I discussing what would happen when our fathers showed up again. How they would make a difference. We dreamed the same dream that our fathers would come and rescue us. We would be taken care of. We would be loved and have everything that the other kids had. Secretly I blamed my mother for my father's absence. It must have been her fault. Every time I went through some bad experience, I blamed my mother for not protecting me.

I wanted out but there was nowhere to go.

I would get myself from Battersea to Acton at only ten years of age. I just wanted my dad to be interested in me and yet he wasn't. I can remember once he picked me up and he had a friend in the car. I was wearing hand-me-down clothes and my dad was angry and embarrassed because the pockets were frayed, yet he never provided for me.

I got caught up in the idealism of my father. One afternoon I turned up at his house and it was the last time I ever saw him. He told me that he was going away to travel through India to find himself. I'm not sure if he managed to find himself but I do know that he never bothered coming back to find me. Before that, I would travel from Battersea to Acton on the other side of London to seek out my father. That started when I was nine or ten. To put this into perspective: I would have to walk a few miles to get on an Overground train then swap to the Underground networks and walk again to reach his flat. Sometimes he was home, sometimes he wasn't. It was clear that he wasn't usually excited to see me. He would sometimes take me home but, more often, he would let me make my own way home.

One time I went to seek out my father and he again expressed his disappointment and embarrassment at the clothes I was wearing. These were the best clothes I owned which were kindly donated to us.

Soon after that, I met a man who showed me affection, something that I did not receive very often. I sacrificed myself to this man for the affection he showed me and was abused by him for some time. I can remember playing outside my home and he would stare down at me from his window. I would go up to his flat. I still can't believe that I would go there and yet anything was better than going back home. Anything was better than witnessing my mother being abused, and whatever that low-life pervert gave to me was better than nothing. I mention this to underline how awful it is living in the confines of domestic abuse. This should never have happened to me or anybody else, and it sickens me that so many children are used in this way. Whatever I had, including my innocence, was taken away from me. I didn't realise that I deserved more. All children deserve more than that. That obviously affected my relationships as a teenager and as an adult.

Around this time I went off the rails and got involved in petty crime. One day I got home and there was a suitcase packed for me and a social worker took me away to an assessment centre. From there I went to 'a boarding school for boys' which was actually a home for disturbed children.

I settled in quite quickly and felt safe there, and whilst you never received any love or affection, I felt safe. It was only when I went home during school holidays that I would get into trouble.

After leaving care at sixteen I was alone. I needed to learn to deal with it but unfortunately I didn't: I got involved in crime and ended up in borstal and then a long prison sentence.

I decided that I was going to change my life and make the best of what was available. Fortunately around this time I met a teacher in prison who believed in me and encouraged me to believe in myself. I put my head down, started listening to classical music to help me concentrate, and got seven O Levels and three A Levels. I also excelled in sport.

Once I got out of prison I had my ups and downs but I have made a success of myself. Don't get me wrong, it's taken a lot of soul-searching and hard work on my behalf, but I am in a good place. I have two beautiful children and am in a loving long-term relationship. I can look at myself these days and feel proud of myself. In spite of being abused I chose not to remain a victim.

What I have learnt over the years is that it's all about choice. Everything is a choice, even to live or die is a choice. Some of the choices are easier to make in life but aren't always the best choices for you. Some choices are a long, hard slog if you want the best. One of the most powerful things I ever learnt was to take responsibility for my actions which has enabled me to move forward with my life.

Having said that, so many people don't understand that they have a choice. Children don't usually have choices because they are at the mercy of those who are supposed to take care of them and guide them through the formative years into adulthood. It only takes one incident to ruin a life.

As an adult, the consequence of the abuse I suffered was that I made many mistakes. Strangely, from not trusting anyone, I found myself giving too much away as deep down I longed to be rescued. I got involved in the wrong relationships. I met a woman shortly after I got out of prison for the last time. The relationship was totally inappropriate. I was twenty-three and Deb was nineteen. We became friends but after a couple of years we developed a sexual relationship. It was quite casual and infrequent but it went on for years. We were both in relationships with other people some of the time, more her than me, but it happened.

Eventually we had a child together. It was an arrangement. Deb was in a long-term lesbian relationship when I got her pregnant. A few years previously to this, she told me that she wanted a child one day and she wanted me to be the father. I was flattered and agreed. I had no idea what I was letting myself in for. It if was today I would run a mile because I would recognise the situation for what it was: unhealthy and bad for me as a person.

I don't believe it was a good choice for her either.

This is a woman who was abused by her uncle. Her father walked out on the family when she was six. Although I understand the reasons for what occurred, I am finding it difficult to forgive her for what came next.

She was cold, sly, calculating and secretive. This is what I didn't see at the time as I didn't know any better. I had nothing to go on. My mum wasn't strong and would let men use her. They got her pregnant and left. She didn't have the self-esteem to realise that she was worth more. She didn't have the courage to stand up for herself and her children.

When she was ready, Deb appeared on my doorstep one day and announced that she was ready to get pregnant. We didn't talk about it. I didn't question it. I didn't see her for a couple of months until she got in touch to tell me that she was pregnant.

Deb was still in a lesbian relationship but her partner had no idea what was happening. She had calculated that her partner would be angry but would go along with it.

Her partner loved her but was also very possessive. I wasn't prepared for the fallout. I became the focus for her lover's anger. What started out as an arrangement where Deb would have our child and I would be involved in his upbringing, became a battle that went on for many years.

After he was born I had to battle for access. I think she had expected me to be a part of his life but her partner did everything in her power to block that. Deb went along with it. My relationship with my son was sacrificed for the sake of her partner's wishes. When challenged, Deb said that she wanted her partner because she would help bring him up. From then on my son was used as a weapon against me. In the end, I am ashamed to say that I gave up.

When my son was six, Deb split from her partner and I was allowed back into his life. I forgave her and was just grateful that I could be a part of his life. Things were good for a while. However, after a couple of years she met another woman who became jealous of my friendship with Deb, and I was pushed out again.

I had to fight again for access. I also discovered that I wasn't on my son's birth certificate. I fought to rectify this but back then, in the nineties, I had no automatic right to be recognised as the father of my child. Deb refused to help me.

Things today are thankfully different for fathers' rights and also for people who are victims of domestic abuse.

I had a partner at the time who was accepting of my relationship with my son but wasn't that interested in him. I was on my own fighting this battle.

While this was going on, I became successful in the entertainment industry and then as a property developer. This brought me a lot of attention and fake friends. I still wasn't getting it. I didn't have the self-esteem or sense enough to know that I was surrounding myself with people that liked me for what I could do for them. I had status and I made a lot of money which I was generous with. I met a woman who I fell in love with. What I didn't realise was that she didn't love me.

Within a year she was pregnant with our daughter. We bought a big house and within two years we were married. Two years after that we were divorced; I lost my home and my business. I also had to endure another child being used against me.

I didn't realise until it was too late that this woman was only interested in what I could provide. I had allowed myself to be used once again.

I sometimes look back and think 'you idiot', but then I realise that I wasn't equipped to do better. I didn't grow up in the right environment and didn't have the guidance or a benchmark to compare to.

I never fail to be appalled when I see or hear about people using their children to hurt their partners or former partners. They become blind to the emotional harm that they cause. It happens far too often and it's unnecessary and just wrong.

Now I am married to a beautiful woman who loves me for who I am, and I love her unconditionally. It took me a long time to get here. I have never been happier. My son is an adult now and we have a great relationship; he is on a good path with his life. He is in a long-term relationship with a good woman who loves him as much as he loves her.

I have learnt to let go and forgive because to hold on to the guilt and continually blame others for where you are at in your life means that you will never be able to move on and will remain the victim living in the past. This has been a lot harder than it sounds. I still struggle sometimes, especially when it comes to my mother. As much as I loved her and understand why she did the things that she did, there is a part of me that finds it difficult to come to terms with.

. . . *Some years ago Petal had made the mistake of sharing a little of Frank's past with Ted. It was while watching an inspiring film that she had turned to Ted and said it reminded her of Frank who, in her eyes, was a hero as against all the odds he'd managed to turn his life around.*

Sadly Ted used this information to hurt them both, telling anyone who would listen about Petal's and Frank's 'dreadful past'. This dirty tactic did little to help Ted's cause but just made him look even more ridiculous.

Petal's and Ted's day in court finally arrived.

Ted looked so handsome in his suit and very confident.

The judge discussed the alcohol result, which had come back fine, and the psychiatric assessment. Ted wanted another psychiatric assessment. He said that Petal's relationship with her psychiatrist would be biased. He wanted an unbiased assessment.

Ted also asked for blood tests, because he knew that her needle phobia would kick in and she would fall apart and display just how 'crazy' she is. Poor Petal started crying and whispered to her barrister: 'I need to leave this now, I can't do this anymore. I'm done. Please, I want to go now.'

Her barrister squeezed her arm and told her to be quiet. The judge glared at Petal for talking and Petal hung her head and listened. Her barrister informed the judge that a hair-strand test was more accurate than a blood test.

The social worker then gave Bluebell's wishes to live on a rolling three-day rota with both of her parents. Petal glared at the social worker. If only she had read all the documentation through in the first place, things would not have escalated as they did. Petal still hadn't got over the encounter with the social worker and the way it had affected her to be told she would lose her daughter and only be allowed supervised visits.

The social worker looked bored and not at all ashamed of herself, which she should've been.

The judge gave his considered decision. He denied Ted's request for yet more psychiatric assessments and alcohol tests. The judge went on to say that it was time that Petal and Bluebell move back home. He would allow Ted three weeks to move out and find himself somewhere else to live.

Ted was furious and his mother was livid, spitting and screaming and making all sorts of accusations. Petal's own poor parents sat in court bewildered and sad but keeping a dignified silence whilst Ted's mother ranted at them.

Petal's barrister congratulated her and told Petal that it was her dignity that won out in the end. 'You refused to stoop to his level, Petal. He dragged you through the depths of hell and yet you still refused to lose your dignity. You should be proud.'

Petal felt bewildered and broken but certainly not proud. She walked away from the court arm in arm with her family, her wonderful friends and Sparkle, the angel from the refuge. Sparkle hugged her and told her she would spread the good news to all the others back at the refuge. She instructed Petal to celebrate . . . and celebrate Petal did!

Frank whisked her off to a wonderful French restaurant. Petal sat there with a grin on her face and holes in her boots but Frank didn't mind that her clothes weren't good enough. Frank accepted Petal for herself, just like her friends who continued to love and support Petal and Bluebell now that they were able to reclaim their home and finally make it their own.

Day One Hundred & Nineteen

Home is where the heart is
Or so some people say
My home's become a toxic cloud
Chasing me away

I stayed with my parents last night. My friend had driven me there. He and my father had loaded the van with the bed and other items they had given me for my daughter, to replace the ones her father was taking.

My friends and family were excited that I was going home, however they knew it was a big step. I hadn't stepped foot in the house for months. My best friend had the keys. We were to meet another friend there to help me clean and move back in.

We were on our way to the house when my best friend called me in tears. She warned me to prepare myself for the condition the house had been left in.

Fortunately my friend had his daughter with him, who was eight at the time. I tried to hide my sadness but she knew I was sad and drew me some beautiful pictures. She made me smile and laugh. I had grown to love her very much.

As I walked through the door I felt as though I was about to pass out. The house was absolutely disgusting. Thank God my own daughter wasn't there and wasn't due back for two days. I would not have wanted her to see her mother's raw pain.

I stood and stared around me. I felt a surreal, floating sensation. It was worse than I had expected. My friends rallied round and started cleaning. They congregated in the kitchen. They made me cups of tea. They hugged me. We aren't huggy types, really, but it came naturally today.

My daughter's room broke my heart. Everything had been removed. Boxes of her stuff had been left but it was pretty much everything she had grown out of and held no sentimental value.

I didn't mind that he had taken almost everything. I had expected all of that to have been taken but what cut to my core was that every photograph, every DVD and every precious gift we had bought our daughter since she was born were gone. He had everything, including my own bicycle and laptop.

My friends worked relentlessly. We collected my dear little puppy. She had been waiting in her crate at my friend's house. She was a gift to me and my daughter. I prayed that the awkwardness between mother and daughter would be masked by this scruffy little dog.

By the end of the day the house smelt fresh and was taking shape. It's amazing how kind people can be. My best friend said that she and her husband were going to buy me a new fridge freezer and another friend and her husband bought me a brand-new washing machine. Someone else had dropped off a sofa and an armchair; his jovial spirit lightened the atmosphere for us all.

It's strange how I had all these wonderful friends who were all so very different from the other, like the most delicious box of chocolates. I was overwhelmed by everyone's kindness. All these exceptional people congregating to help me and my daughter.

Then came the hard bit. They all needed to go home. My friend said he would run his daughter home to her mother and then he would come and sleep at the house with me.

That must have been one of the longest few hours of my life, waiting for him to come back.

My sweet little dog sat in her enormous crate staring at me. I'm sure she was trying to read my mind. I got her out yet again and cuddled her. Like the brown paper bag I had been breathing into for months, she seemed to calm me down.

My friend got back; he bought wine and a takeaway. He was the kindest man I had ever met. He had his own beautiful home in London and yet here he was camping out at my house.

He stayed until my daughter returned to start her rolling three-day rota. He promised to return when she went back to her father.

I was so nervous about seeing my daughter. I couldn't wait to see her and yet I was petrified. Not only could I see the pain my daughter was in but I could feel it. I desperately wanted to hold her in my arms and stroke her hair and apologise over and over for all she was going through, but I knew it was the last thing she wanted.

. . . *Petal knows that Ted's legacy will remain inside her forever, but also that time is a great healer.*

Her priority now is the message she needs to deliver to Bluebell.

She prays each and every day that dear little Bluebell will learn from her own childhood experiences and in time will seek out a partner, a soul mate who will help her grow and become the free spirit all human beings have a right to be.

Day One Hundred & Twenty-Two

I'm struggling to be here
I'm scared to be alone
Kind and pretty fairies
Building me a home

My friends spent weeks helping me paint the house. They brought carpet cleaners, paint brushes and spent hours doing my daughter's bedroom and the bathroom.

My friend's husband grouted the kitchen tiles and re-grouted the bathroom tiles.

They helped me clean my windows and leant me items for my daughter.

I was so overwhelmed by their kindness.

My home was beginning to take on a new atmosphere and one which hinted at possibilities of happiness.

DAY ONE HUNDRED & THIRTY-FOUR

Pandora has refused to help
She says I'll never win
She has left the contents of her box
Now the walls are caving in

The 'understanding relationships' course has come to an end so soon and I'm devastated. I was just getting going. Pandora's Box has been well and truly prised open, exposing so many secrets that I cannot seem to walk three paces without tripping over something. I know that it may be unsettling, but I'm aware that I need to go through the box carefully, as I honestly believe that it is the only route to freedom. For that very reason I want to continue sharing my story with these amazing women, as each and every story shared helps to heal another.

We have all learnt a lot about ourselves and one thing that has occurred to me during this time is just how lucky I am to have friends and the solid support around me. I tingle as I think of the women's refuge and of the wonderful women who work there. I can no longer refer to them as the 'unbroken angels' as I realise I have no idea who they really are. It's about the kindness of strangers, I guess. Anyway, broken or unbroken, it matters not. They are incredible without exception.

I shudder when I think of the social worker who almost changed the course of my life and my daughter's, too. Time and again I hear stories of social services ripping apart the very families they are meant to protect.

I vow that I owe it to myself, my daughter and my amazing support network to help other victims of physical, sexual and mental domestic abuse. To give something back in the hope that it will help others.

Without my friends and the professionals who got involved I know I would never have got through this torture.

Thank you all from the bottom of my heart.

Day Six Hundred & Fifty-Three (Aftermath)

RUN

I see you, everywhere I turn you are here.
They say, 'it's only four walls, let him go'
But they don't know that within these walls you still live,
Entrenched under the paint, within the plaster.

Memories haunt me day and night,
Some are happy, these make me miss you and sad.
Some are sad, they still make me sad.
Some are frightening, I'm still so scared I need to run.

I spent years running away from you,
Hoping the distance would bridge the gap.
I could never please you, so I ran further away
You showed no mercy, I ran further, stayed away longer.

You are gone now but your presence still lingers.
You pulsate, like a throbbing vein each time the house falls
quiet.
I can hear you, I can see you, I can feel you wherever I turn.
I flee the house and drive or walk, although you're gone I still
need to run.

Since leaving the refuge I have had a great deal to think about as I started my crawl back to life. I still meet with the two managers (unless of course one of them selfishly takes a break and goes on holiday!). All joking aside, they are incredible. It has been a long time since I left the refuge and yet still their support continues. Some weeks I pop in just for a coffee and a giggle; others it's because I'm back to breathing into the paper bag, and they help me dissect the main cause of my anxiety and gently steer me out and on my way again. No two weeks are the same at the refuge, but the one thing that does remain the same is their unbelievable strength, their never-ending patience and understanding, and they really are two of the funniest women I have ever met in my life.

Since leaving the refuge and moving back home, I have been able to establish exactly what meeting these incredible women has done for me. My anxiety levels are still high and I am fighting with all my strength to conquer it. As the managers recently explained to me, 'You've spent years, decades, in a high state of anxiety. It won't just miraculously disappear. It's going to take hard work.'

Between the two managers, my GP and psychotherapist, I have quite an awesome support network, offering expert advice.

I spent years worrying about leaving my ex-partner for the effect it would have on my daughter. For years my closest friends listened patiently as I voiced my fear at staying, yet my fear of leaving him. They, too, felt it better for my daughter's sake that we stay together as a family, but we were all so wrong.

I have learnt that domestic abuse should not be tolerated by anyone, and no child should be expected to live amongst such poison; otherwise it could seep through the pores into their skin until it becomes part of their soul, too.

On the rare occasions I have flown on a plane, the advice was given that should the plane encounter trouble and oxygen is required, it is recommended the mother place the mask over her own mouth first and put on her life jacket before tending to her child. It hadn't made much sense to me at the time until my mother explained it to me: in order to keep the child safe, the mum would need to be safe, calm and coherent to protect her child and help them and comfort them.

I realise that the refuge uses the same tactics. They put the mother first (whilst giving as much love and support as they can to the children), because they know if they can support the mother and make her strong and healthy and safe, if they can make her see herself as worthwhile and special, then she will hopefully be able to give the same to her children.

Whilst I was in refuge another woman came in with two children. She was so angry, so broken that it seemed no-one wanted to be near her, including her own children. Just having her walk into the communal lounge would be intimidating. Even a couple of members of the staff had appeared nervous around her. The managers, however, refused to quit. They refused to give up on her.

A few weeks into her stay and the transformation in this woman was nothing short of a miracle. I remember one evening my daughter saying, 'Mummy, listen.' The woman was bathing her child and the laughter and splashing coming from them both was captivating.

I had watched the managers painstakingly trying to get her to join in the organised events. They dedicated hours to talking to her and listening to her. They saw something the rest of us couldn't see – a beautiful, strong woman – and they gently steered her until she came face to face with herself, to the 'self' before the years of abuse. A woman who cared, who was funny and kind. A woman whose love was infectious; and her children blossomed with her right before our eyes.

I often think of her now and the other broken angels I met. How are they coping, now they are on the outside, I wonder?

GHOSTS

The managers constantly reassure me now as I stumble around my life, amongst all the ghosts, the guilt, the fear and confusion. They listen to my endless questions . . .

I ask myself whether perhaps if I had made a fresh start away from the family home, would it have been easier? Yes, it would, of course it would. That is one thing I am certain of, but why should I lose my beautiful home? Why should I take my daughter from the home she has grown up in and away perhaps from our friends? Surely I have lost so much already? I lost years of being with my parents and friends. I lost years of being allowed a natural relationship with my daughter. Why should I now lose the one place that has felt like home since leaving my childhood home over thirty years ago?

When I tell the managers that I am concerned by how much of their time I still take up, they reassure me that they are here for as long as I need them and that I don't have to be on my knees to see them.

Domestic abuse really does seep into your soul and unfortunately taints it. I had naïvely thought that by removing myself and my daughter from an abusive environment that things would miraculously get better and, as if by magic, I would be all fixed. Sadly I was mistaken. However, what I have learnt is that I am determined to get beyond this and I am in a much better place than I was a few years ago, and so is my daughter, in spite of living a rather transient life.

QUESTION: WHY DIDN'T I JUST...?

Answer: I felt so sorry for him. He made me feel responsible for all that had gone wrong in our relationship.

He accepted no responsibility whatsoever.

That was one of the most frightening days, when I realised that he genuinely believed he was the victim in all this and that he was not behaving inappropriately. I know that he still believes he is the victim. He still believes I ruined his life when, in truth, I think he is far happier now that we are not together, but I know he will never, ever admit it. I wish he could let go of the anger and bitterness, for his own sake as well as for our daughter. I still live in hope that one day he will be able to acknowledge his behaviour and seek help to find happiness.

Sadly I am not sure that day will come, because nothing was ever his fault.

I remember asking him one afternoon, to picture a man in a few years' time treating our daughter like he was treating me. I asked him how he would feel to see his daughter being treated so badly. He had stared at me defiantly and said he would question what his daughter had done to her partner to make the man treat her like that.

Answer: Love . . . I guess for many years it was because I loved him. I loved him so much.

Answer: Guilt . . . I felt so guilty. I truly believed for years that I had taken that beautiful man and destroyed his life. My anxiety disorder made me a nightmare to live with and it drove him crazy. How often he would tell me and my daughter that: 'Because of Mummy we can't go anywhere'; 'Daddy wants to take you on a proper holiday but we can't because of Mummy'; 'If only you had known me years ago, you would have seen a very different Daddy. I used to be so different.'

When my panic attacks occurred, he would be embarrassed by me drawing attention to myself and him, so he refused to go anywhere with me; and he wasn't keen on me taking our daughter anywhere either.

Answer: Belief . . . When I was pregnant with our daughter, my anxiety levels had spiralled. In hindsight I believe it was partly due to being isolated from my friends and family.

My ex-partner attended an appointment with my old GP, my psychotherapist, a psychiatrist and my community psychiatric nurse (CPN). When he returned home he was extremely anxious and angry. He told me how they had wanted to put me into an acute psychiatric unit as they weren't happy with me being left alone. He told me how the baby was to be born in the hospital and that they would keep us there. I remember how he ranted and raved that his child was going to be born in a loony bin and that he knew they would never let the baby or me out. He said that they would keep us there. After he had built up the horrific picture of my future, he then proudly announced that he had been able to persuade them all that he could take care of me and the baby. So it was agreed that I would be allowed to stay out of the acute psychiatric unit. Then came the massive announcement: only on condition that we be released into his care.

I was terrified of being locked away. I was so grateful to him for saving me and our unborn child. He really was the hero of all heroes.

I believed him. I never once questioned it. It was only during the final stages of our court hearings that I saw he had put the account in his statement. I asked my CPN (who had since become a cherished friend) about it. She had looked shocked and was horrified that I had actually believed him. She informed me that the 'acute psychiatric hospital' was actually a mother and baby ward at a standard hospital. She said that there were never any discussions about putting me in a psychiatric unit and there was never any agreement that I was released into his care.

She said the meeting was held simply to make sure they had plenty of support in place for me.

Day One Thousand & Thirty-Two

The bogeyman lingers,
refusing to go.
I can still see him now
And only I know.

Recently someone asked me: 'What was the worst bit?'
They asked me: 'How do you get beyond that stuff?'
It made me realise that I haven't . . . not really . . .

I had underestimated the devastating effect my relationship has had on me. It's been three years since I left the refuge and yet not one day goes by that I don't miss being there. When I was there I was in limbo, but a safe limbo, with the knowledge that I was cared for and supported.

Don't get me wrong, I still have all the support in the world, but I genuinely thought that the easy bit was going back home with my daughter and, just like the movie I once watched, everything would miraculously become perfect. The sun would shine forever and the fairies would fly around our heads sprinkling their fairy dust over us to protect us and make sure we were safe and happy.

However, back in the real world . . .

How Has It Affected Me?

Living as a victim of domestic abuse was actually easier for me than dealing with the aftermath of it all. Living in that environment made me feel helpless and powerless. When you are being so controlled, you are so preoccupied with coping with it that it helps you focus. It gives you strict discipline and lines you know never to cross. It was a slow process. But there were so many happy moments. We shared our beautiful daughter. I was so in love with him. He said he loved me. He said it was in the name of love.

Apparently I was to blame . . .

If I was ill it was my own fault. I wasn't going to the toilet enough. I wasn't eating the right foods. I wasn't drinking enough water, or orange juice . . . He wasn't getting on at me, it was because he loved me. It was for my own good.

I am certain that he still blames my daughter when she is ill, for picking up germs, for not washing her hands enough, for not constantly using antibacterial hand gel, for placing her towel too close to other people's, for wiping her toothbrush against the neck of the toothpaste where other toothbrushes touch. He isn't getting on at her, it's because he loves her that he is telling her this. It's for her own good – just like he did to me.

If she gets poorly, he gets poorly; she infects him – just like I did to him.

I remember how he would say on a regular basis, 'Look at

Mummy, look at Mummy's posture; do you want to end up like that?'

Is it any wonder I always feel like the hunchback of Notre Dame?

I remember his constant criticism: 'Look at Mummy's hair, how she's ruined it. Do you want hair like Mummy's?'

Funny, I hate my hair these days.

I also remember how I wasn't allowed to choose any clothes for our daughter. Simple little things and yet they crushed my spirit.

Why did I stay so long? Those last few years, of course, were because he refused to leave my home and I had nowhere else to go that wasn't miles away from my daughter. But before I fell out of love, before that awful moment when I discovered I was being abused, why stay?

Now I feel differently. I can see things a little clearer. This man believed he was in love with me and I believed him. This man dedicated his life to caring about me. From his obsession with my mental health issues to my posture, my clothes, my health, my hygiene, my cooking, my cleaning, my career, my mothering skills, my friends, my family. All of it I was doing wrong and he pointed it out to help me, because he loved me.

I'm still saddened through to my core that I was gullible enough to believe it was in the name of love. And yes! I hand-on-heart believed it.

When I recently voiced my fears for my daughter to one of the refuge managers, I explained that my daughter was clearly afraid to stand up to her father. The refuge manager asked: 'What would you like to happen? What would you like your daughter to do differently?'

I said, 'I want her to get angry. I want her to stand up to him.'

The refuge manager smiled kindly and reminded me: 'But you

know how hard it is to stand up to him, you never could and I guess she's struggling too.'

'Oh my God, it's my fault, isn't it? She's copying me.'

'You did stand up to him,' the refuge manager reminded me. 'In the end you left him. You showed your daughter that she has two feet stuck on the end of her legs and until she chooses to use them and vote with her feet then I'm afraid there's not a lot you can do. You taught her a valuable lesson.'

I wonder how many other fifteen-year-old girls or boys live within such a stifling environment with a mother or a father or a partner who lords it around them, controlling them, bullying them and basking in their imaginary power.

Broken Angels has never felt more real to me. It has never felt more important than it does today and I am determined to get it out there to reach anyone who needs to hear and will listen.

WHERE AM I NOW?

I have found a beautiful clearing. There's a waterfall. The sun is shining. There are the most beautiful colours: flowers, birds, animals. I can now see my beautiful friends and family. I can't always join in with them all but at least I can sit and watch them, enjoying them.

My beautiful daughter laughs a lot these days and often stops what she is doing and comes over and sits beside me. We hug, we laugh together. We are closer now than we have ever been. She knows I am doing everything in my power to get up and go over and join in but she is patient. She knows I love her and I know she loves me. She accepts her oddball and misfit of a mother. She accepts that I may never be able to join in wholeheartedly, but she knows that I will try with every ounce of my being, and I know if I can't then she will accept me for who I am.

THE BROKEN ANGELS
BY THE ELDER

We are the Broken Angels, we've forgotten how to cry,
We broke our wings, we broke our hearts when we fell from the sky.
We've been dragged down to hell and back . . .
You can see it in our eyes.
Please fix these sadly wounded wings, we'll show you how we fly.

When I fled my home, I had to go,
This time there was no choice.
Despair and humiliation finally broke my inner voice.
Would an innocent young loved one become affected just like me?
So I became the exile . . . the 'Broken' refugee.

We are the Broken Angels, we've forgotten how to cry,
We broke our wings, we broke our hearts when we fell from the sky.
We've been dragged down to hell and back . . .
You can see it in our eyes.
Please fix these sadly wounded wings, we'll show you how we fly.

If you're a Broken Angel,
And you don't know what to do.
Seek help from the 'Refuge', they'll take good care of you.

Where they ask the tender questions,
And won't tell you any lies,

But they'll nurture and protect you . . .
And give you back your eyes.

I was the Broken Angel, I'd forgotten how to cry,
I broke my wings, I broke my heart when I fell from the sky.
I've been dragged down to hell and back
This comes as a surprise . . .
My wings now work, my eyes now see, it's time for me to fly.

Appendix 1
Women's Refuge UK
written by The Managers

The accounts contained within *Broken Angels* highlight the experiences of so many women, men and children who have lived with domestic violence and abuse and their incredible bravery in breaking free.

It is a privilege and honour for us to witness the incredible journey of so many women and children who have come through our services, as they have moved away from violence and abuse and started to reclaim their lives and recover from the devastating impact of the abuse.

The cross-government definition of domestic violence and abuse is: any incident or pattern of incidents of controlling, coercive, threatening behaviour, violence or abuse between those aged 16 or over who are, or have been, intimate partners or family members regardless of gender or sexuality. The abuse can encompass, but is not limited to:

- psychological
- physical
- sexual
- financial
- emotional

Controlling Behaviour
Controlling behaviour is a range of acts designed to make a person

subordinate and/or dependent by isolating them from sources of support, exploiting their resources and capacities for personal gain, depriving them of the means needed for independence, resistance and escape, and regulating their everyday behaviour.

Coercive Behaviour
Coercive behaviour is an act or a pattern of acts of assault, threats, humiliation and intimidation or other abuse that is used to harm, punish, or frighten their victim.

The changes to the definition of domestic abuse raise awareness that young people in the 16 to 17 age group can also be victims of domestic violence and abuse.

There continues to be some shocking statistics relating to domestic violence and abuse:

- Each year an estimated 1.9m people in the UK suffer some form of domestic abuse – 1.3 million female victims (8.2% of the population) and 600,000 male victims (4%)
- Each year more than 100,000 people in the UK are at high and imminent risk of being murdered or seriously injured because of domestic abuse
- Women are much more likely than men to be the victims of high risk or severe domestic abuse: 95% of those going to MARAC or accessing an IDVA service are women
- In 2013–14 the police recorded 887,000 domestic abuse incidents in England and Wales
- Seven women a month are killed by a current or former partner in England and Wales
- 130,000 children live in homes where there is high-risk domestic abuse
- 62% of children living with domestic abuse are directly harmed by the perpetrator of the abuse, in addition to the

harm caused by witnessing the abuse of others

- On average high-risk victims live with domestic abuse for 2.3 years before getting help
- 85% of victims sought help five times on average from professionals in the year before they got effective help to stop the abuse

Sources

CAADA (2014), In Plain Sight: Effective help for children exposed to domestic abuse. Bristol: CAADA.

ONS (2016), March 2015 Crime Survey for England and Wales (CSEW).

SafeLives (2015), Getting it right first time: policy report. Bristol: SafeLives.

SafeLives (2015), Insights IDVA National Dataset 2013–14. Bristol: SafeLives.

SafeLives (2014), MARAC national dataset 2014. Bristol: SafeLives.

Children are often the hidden victims of domestic violence and abuse. It has a particularly detrimental effect as they are reliant upon their parents to provide love and support, as well as to be responsible for practicalities. When domestic violence occurs, the family, which should be a safe and secure haven and the main support in their lives, becomes a source of trauma, division and pain.

Children can 'experience domestic abuse' in a variety of ways. For example, they may be in the same room and may even get caught in the middle of an incident; they may be in the next room and hear the abuse or see their mother's physical injuries.

It is easy to assume that children who are not directly involved in the abuse are not affected. However, I am sure that you are aware that children can sense tension and insecurity and this can only have a detrimental influence on their development.

With these continuing statistics, it is vital that the silence, shame and stigma of domestic abuse and violence continues to be challenged, and the vital work of domestic abuse services continues.

Appendix 2
Sources Of Help

Women's Aid National Helpline
Women's Aid is the national charity for women and children working to end domestic abuse.
Tel: 0808 2000 247 24-hour helpline.

Childline
24-hour confidential listening service for children.
Tel: 0800 1111
www.childline.org.uk

NSPCC
Advice for adults who are worried about a child.
Tel: 0800 800 5000 (24 hours)
www.nspcc.org.uk

Respond
Support for Disabled Survivors.
Tel: 0808 8080700 (limited opening hours)

Professional Counselling
Grace Counselling
email: grace4counselling@gmail.com

Forced Marriage Helpline
Tel: 0800 5999 247 (not 24 hours)

Rape Crisis
National body that provides co-ordination for the rape crisis movement in England and Wales.
www.rapecrisis.org.uk (lists local centres)

Broken Rainbow
A service for lesbian, gay, bisexual and transsexual people who are experiencing domestic violence (run in partnership with London Lesbian and Gay Switchboard).
Tel: 08452 60 44 60 (limited opening hours)

MALE
Support for male victims of domestic abuse. Men's advice line and enquiries.
Tel: 0808 801 0327
www.mensadviceline.org.uk

Rights of Women
Free Legal Advice.
Tel: 020 7251 6577 or textphone: 020 7490 2562
www.rightsofwomen.org.uk

FORWARD
Support and advice about female genital mutilation.
Tel: 0208 960 4000

National Forced Marriage Unit
Help for those who have been forced into marriage overseas; are at risk of being forced into marriage; or people worried about friends or relatives.
Tel: 0207 008 0151

Imkaan

A national charity dedicated to the development of the specialist Asian women's refuge sector.

www.imkaan.org.uk

Southall Black Sisters

Support, advocacy and information to Asian and African Caribbean women experiencing abuse (London based).

www.southallblacksisters.org.uk

Poppy Project

Support and housing for women trafficked into prostitution (London based).

www.eaves4women.co.uk/POPPY_ Project/POPPY_Project.php

Appendix 3
Psychotherapy

(What does it mean to me?)
Abigail Sinclair

I sat, not unlike a mangled, twisted ball of wool.

I had spent hours, days, years, desperately trying to unravel it and yet it just got more and more mangled.

The more mangled it got, the more desperate I became.

The more desperate I became, the more frustration and anger I felt, to the point where I wanted to throw it onto a fire where I no longer had to look at it.

Psychotherapists offered to help unravel it.

I didn't believe they could, but anything was worth a try, otherwise it would of been of no use to anyone, least of all me.

So, years later the wool is unravelled, it did need cutting at times and carefully knotted back together again.

I look at it now. I can see the knots, I can feel them. Its slightly grubby where our hands have got hot and frustrated, trying to move it, stretch it. cut it and knot it.

I understand that the wool may never be perfect enough to use in all its glory, to create the perfect sweater or scarf, however, It's at least 'together' and I can use it for other, less perfect creations and I will never ever let it go because my psychotherapist taught me that with patience, you can untangle the complexities of your life.

Through their patience and wisdom, a psychotherapist can gently guide you to an understanding of your self worth understanding.

Sarah Grace Counselling and Psychotherapy

Contact Sarah Grace, Reg. MBACP Pg,Dip Psychotherapist.
Email: grace4counselling@gmail.com

Acknowledgements

My thanks go to the women's refuge: the managers, my outreach worker, and to all the amazing staff who work there.

To the Portman Clinic. The Tavistock Clinic.

To my psychotherapist who spends each week with me, patiently trying to help me to keep going.

To my amazing GP who still dedicates hours of her time each year to supporting and protecting me. No-one could ask for more than she gives.

There were many times when I longed to give up but these people carried me through, getting angry on my behalf or just holding me whilst I cried.

I would also like to thank: My parents. Allan and Barbara. Pat Craven. My solicitor and barrister.

Thank you to Sarah Grace and Malcolm Down. For the care they have taken of me, for believing in me and for publishing Broken Angels.

Thank you to my beautiful friends, old and new who, for protection reasons I cannot name but you all know who you are. You all helped me get through.

To my best friend who stood shoulder to shoulder throughout.

I thank the lovely man I am now married to for being solid and patient. I also thank him for proving that there really is equality in a relationship and for showing me unconditional love.

Finally, to my beautiful, funny, brave daughter who travels beside me. In spite of all she has been through, she is incredibly kind and patient. She asks for nothing. She expects nothing and yet is grateful for everything.

I dedicate this journal to them all.

There is a woman who sadly I never got to meet. A woman whose life was stained by domestic abuse. By meeting a member of her family I have had the honour of hearing her story. She had none of the support I enjoyed and yet she turned her life around and made the abuse stop. I carry her story in my heart and on the days that grew dark and I felt like giving up, I would remind myself that she did it alone, and I dug deeper and carried on.